Elnathan John is one of Nigeria's r
satirists. He has twice been shortl
Prize for African Writing (2013 & 2015). His writing has been
published in *Per Contra, Evergreen Review* and Chimurenga's
The Chronic. His debut novel, *Born on a Tuesday*, won a Betty
Trask Award in 2017 and was shortlisted for the Nigeria
Prize for Literature. He is a judge for the 2019 Man Booker
International Prize.

BE(COM)ING NIGERIAN: ~~A GUIDE~~

Elnathan John

Abuja – London

First published in 2019 by Cassava Republic Press

Abuja – London

First published in the USA in 2020 by Cassava Republic Press

Some parts of this book have previously appeared in different forms in Daily Trust Newspapers, ZAM Magazine, Daily Times of Nigeria, The Guardian (UK) and The Africa Report.

A CIP catalogue record for this book is available from the National Library of Nigeria and British Library.

ISBN: 978-1-911115-96-0

eISBN: 978-1-911115-97-7

Book design by Tobi Ajiboye

Cover & Art Direction by Seyi Adegoke

Printed and bound in Great Britian by Clays Ltd, Elcograf S.p.A.

Distributed in Nigeria by Yellow Danfo

Distributed in the UK by Central Books Ltd.

Distributed in the US by Consortium Books

Stay up to date with the latest books, special offers and
exclusive content with our monthly newsletter.
Sign up on our website:
www.cassavarepublic.biz
Twitter: @cassavarepublic
Instagram: @cassavarepublicpress
Facebook: facebook.com/CassavaRepublic
Hashtag: #BecomingNigerian #ReadCassava

To all who feel personally attacked or offended by
something in this book,

With love.

ACKNOWLEDGEMENTS

I'd like to acknowledge Nigeria, with whom I am (still) in an abusive relationship.

Table of Contents

INTRODUCTION

Never, ever, explain satire.
— Elnathan John, 2019.

IN THE BEGINNING…

THE GOSPEL ACCORDING TO NIGERIA

Chapter 1

[1]In the beginning the British created the Northern and Southern protectorates. Now, the nation was formless and empty and darkness covered our collective identity. [2]And the British said: 'Let there be Nigeria.' And there was Nigeria. And the British saw that Nigeria was good (for them) and they separated the ruling class from the serfs. [3]And the British said: 'Just as we have a vault between us and you, let there be a vault to separate the rulers from the citizens.' [4]So the British created Nigeria in their own image, in the image of their colonial rulership they created it; oppressor and oppressed they created them. [5]And there was independence from the British and there were coups and counter coups and there were military dictators. [6]And the decades passed and the military rulers stripped their garbs and uniforms and transformed into civilian rulers. And they declared: 'Old things have passed away and all things have become new.'

Chapter 2

[1]For our military dictators loved the country so much that they gave up their only begotten uniforms and the right to make

decrees, that whosoever believed in them and voted for them should be stuck with them until their old age.

Chapter 3

[1]And it came about that a usurper who was not a military dictator found his way to the throne, through natural deaths and impeachments, and he came upon Nigerians like a thief in the night. [2]And he came not to build but to steal and destroy. And he left Nigerians blind and poor. [3]And Nigerians looked to a former dictator and said to him: 'Lord, we know not where we are going.' [4]And he answered them and said: 'I am the way, the truth and the life. No one comes to good governance except through me.' [5]And he gained followers and drove out the usurper who had left Nigerians blind and poor. [6]And his followers said: 'Lord show us the way and that will be enough for us. Show us Change.' [7]And he answered them and said: 'Do you believe that I am good governance and good governance is me? You may ask for anything in my name and I will do it.' [8]And his followers worshipped him and sang his praises day and night. [9]And when his ministers proved incompetent, his followers praised him and denounced the ministers. [10]And when the people began to groan under much suffering, they looked unto their benevolent dictator. [11]And he said to them: 'If you love me, keep my commands. Hate those who hate me and love those who love me. My enemies cannot accept me, because they neither see me nor know me. But you know me, for I live with you and will be in you.' [12]And some sceptics said, 'But, Lord, why do your ministers in 2018 do silly things like wear silly red berets and have nothing under the berets?' [13]And the benevolent dictator replied, 'Anyone who loves me will obey my teaching. Anyone who does not love me will not obey my teaching.'

Chapter 4

[1]For the shameless will inherit the land and they will dwell in it in an abundance of peace. [2]For the shameless, instead of shame there shall be a double portion; for the wicked and corrupt instead of dishonour, they shall rejoice in their lot; they shall have everlasting joy and in their old age be called elder statesmen. [3]And the last shall be the first.

Chapter 5

[1]If I fight for the human rights of random individuals or of enemies of the Lord but do not have loyalty to the benevolent dictator, I am only a resounding gong or a clanging cymbal. If I have the gift of turning the economy around and can fathom all the mysteries of the parallel market and if I am angry that pilgrims get dollars and not business men and women but do not have loyalty to the dictator and love for him, I am nothing. [2]Love is patient (with inefficiency), love is kind (even in the face of massacres). It does not envy the benevolent dictator, it does not boast that it can do better. It is not proud. [3]Love keeps no record of wrongs, whether those wrongs happened in 1984 and are being repeated or those wrongs lead to hundreds of people being secretly buried. [4]Love does not delight in evil except where that evil happens to people we do not like, such as strange ethnic groups or religions or sexualities. [5]But love rejoices with the truth: and the truth is what the benevolent dictator says it is. [6]Love always protects the interest of the dictator and blames only his ministers for things that go wrong. [7]Love never fails. [8]But where there is common sense, it will cease. Whether there are industries, they will cease. Where there is electricity, it will reduce. And where there is a great football team, it will diminish. Where there are cheap dollars, they will be reserved for pilgrims and

billionaires. [9]For we know in part and we pontificate through newspaper articles and blogs in part, but when completeness through our benevolent dictator (and his minions) arrives, what is in part disappears.

Chapter 6

[1]The benevolent dictator is my shepherd, I shall lack nothing. [2]He makes me lie down in hunger and fear, but only because it leads me to righteousness. [3]He refreshes my soul. [4]He guides me along his own paths for his name's sake. [5]Even though I walk through the darkest valley with no electricity, I will fear no evil, for he is with me. [6]His rod and his staff with which he makes hundreds of Shiites disappear, they comfort me.

Chapter 7

[1]Blessed are [those who steal from] the poor in spirit, for theirs is the kingdom of political rebirths. [2]Blessed are those who [make others like Shiites] mourn, for they will be comforted [by the silence of dead and putrefied bodies]. [3]Blessed are [those who despise] the meek for they will inherit the earth. [4]Blessed are those with good political alliances, for even when they are caught, they will be shown mercy. [5]Blessed are [those who hate] the pure in heart, for they will see the inner walls of the Villa. [6]Blessed are those who trend political hashtags, for theirs is the kingdom of bank alerts. [7]Blessed are the kidnappers, for their ransom money will come intact and without repercussion. [8]Blessed are those with a long career of theft and destruction, for they will be called elder statesmen.

Chapter 8

[1]The benevolent dictator gathered all his disciples and taught them a new prayer. He said, [2]You must pray then this way: [3]Our Father, who art Aliko, hallowed be thy wealth [4]Thy

monopolies come [5]Thy will be done in this government as it was in the previous [ones] [6]Give us this day, your refinery (as we give you our cheap dollars) [7]Forgive us our suspicions as we have forgiven those who are suspicious of us [8]And lead us not into temptation to break your monopolies (and empower other entrepreneurs), but deliver us from the evil ones who challenge [y]our government. [9]For thine is the sugar, the flour and the cement (and rice and spaghetti), forever and ever, Amen.'

SPIRITUAL

HOW TO WORSHIP THE NIGERIAN GOD

The Nigerian God is one. It may have various manifestations, but it is essentially different sides of the same coin. Sometimes, adherents of the different sides may fight and kill each other. But Nigerians all worship the Nigerian God.

For all those who want to become better worshipers, this is for you.

If you are a new or prospective convert, this is how you must serve him in your day to day life. You will be richly blessed for choosing the Nigerian God. (And in case you were wondering, yes, the Nigerian God is a full-blooded Nigerian male).

The prayer

First, let me clarify: a few people confuse being a worshiper with complicated things like character, good work or righteousness. The fact that you choose to open every meeting with multiple prayers does not mean that you intend to do what is right. It nonetheless means that the opening prayer is important. Nothing, I repeat nothing, can work without it. If you are gathered to discuss how to inflate contracts, begin with an opening prayer or two. If you are gathered to discuss how to rig elections, begin with a prayer. The Nigerian God appreciates communication.

When you sneak away from your wife to call your girlfriend in the bathroom, and she asks if you will come this weekend, you must say — in addition to "Yes" — "By God's grace" or "God willing" or "insha Allah". It doesn't matter what language you use. Just say it. The Nigerian God likes to be consulted before you do anything, including a trip to Obudu to see one of your [other] lovers. Sometimes, when you have impressed one of your many lovers with your sexual prowess and they look at you in amazement, just say: 'Baby, I give God all the glory.'

The loudspeaker

When worshipping the Nigerian God, be loud. No, the Nigerian God is not hard of hearing. He just appreciates your loud fervour, like he appreciates loud raucous music. The Nigerian God doesn't care if you have neighbours and neither should you. When you are worshipping in your house, make sure the neighbours can't sleep. Use loudspeakers even if there are only two of you in the building. Anyone who complains must be evil. God will judge such a person.

Enemies

This is how the Nigerian God judges people who are your enemies — evil people who want to spoil your hustle; your colleagues who don't want your promotion; your single old aunties who secretly don't want you to marry that rich handsome man (who you haven't met yet); your neighbours who are blocking you spiritually from getting pregnant — He consumes them by fire. He returns all their evil plans to sender. So, when making requests about all your enemies, do not pray that they be forgiven or that they change. Pray that the Nigerian God kills them off in a blazing, holy fire.

Attribution

Attribute everything to the Nigerian God. So, if you diverted funds from public projects and you are able to afford that new Mercedes, when people say you have a nice car, say, 'Na God'. If someone asks what the secret of all your wealth is, say, 'God has been good to me' or 'My God is faithful'. By this you mean the Nigerian God who gave you the uncommon wisdom to re-appropriate public funds.

Consult the Nigerian God when you don't feel like working. The Nigerian God understands that we live in a harsh climate where it is hard to do any real work. So, if you have no clue how to be in charge and things start collapsing, ask people to pray to God and ask for his intervention.

Elections

The Nigerian God loves elections and politics. When you have bribed people to get the Party nomination, used thugs to steal and stuff ballot boxes, intimidated people into either sitting at home or voting for you, lied about everything from your assets to your age, and you eventually (through God's grace) win the election, you must begin by declaring that your success is the will of the almighty and living God and that the other candidate should accept this will of God. Mere mortals should not complain about who God chooses to reward with political success.

Respect

The Nigerian God does not tolerate disrespect. If someone insults your religion, you must look for anyone like them and kill them. It doesn't matter what you use — sticks, machetes, grenade launchers, IED's, AK47's. The Nigerian God sometimes appreciates a good beheading for people who blaspheme. If the person who insults your religion is online and you can't locate them, feel free to threaten to kill them. Like we say: "at all-at all na im bad pass". Something is better than nothing at all.

Miracles

The Nigerian God performs signs and wonders. He does everything from curing HIV to high blood pressure. And the Nigerian God is creative: he can teach a person who was born blind the difference between blue and green when the man of God asks, and he can teach a person born deaf instant English. As a worshipper you must let him deliver you because every case of sickness is caused by evil demons and not infections. Every case of infertility for example is caused by witches and demons and not things like endometriosis or low sperm motility. So instead of hospital, visit agents of the Nigerian God.

PS. The Nigerian God does not cure corruption. Do not attempt to mock him.

Money

The Nigerian God loves money. Because money answereth all things. You know how Nigeria is — things may be difficult, but they are always possible with money. You can get everything:

healthcare, security, clean water, electricity, love, and miracles, when you have money. The Nigerian God knows this and tries to crowdfund in the event of a demand for miracles. So, no, please, don't mess with the Nigerian God's money stream. Don't blaspheme by challenging things like tithes. Who will pay for that private jet or the mansions and cars?

The Internet

If you worship the Nigerian God, you are under no obligation to be nice or kind to people who are not worshippers. They deserve no courtesy.

The Nigerian God is also online. As a worshipper, you are not obliged to be good or decent on Facebook or Twitter all week except on Friday and Sunday, both of which the Nigerian God marks as holy. So, you may forward obscene photos, insult people, pass on lewd jokes all days except the Nigerian holy days. On those holy days, put up statuses saying how you are crazy about God.

The Nigerian God also permits tweets and Facebook updates like: "Now in Church" or "This guy in front of me needs to stop dozing" when performing acts of worship. Also, there is nothing like a Twitter hashtag with your pastor's Sunday sermon: #SundaysWithJesus #JesusRocks #SundaySermon #Crazy4JC.

In all, the Nigerian God is very kind and accommodating. He gives glory and riches and private jets. And if you worship him well, he will immensely bless your hustle.

HOW TO BE A PASTOR

So, you have learnt how to worship the Nigerian God but you want to take it a step further and serve Him more fully. Being a pastor is one of the most rewarding things you can do as a Nigerian. Here is how to do it:

Fly private.

A man of God should not suffer any discomfort while doing the work of the Lord. That is why you are rightly called a man of God. You are too divine to spend time waiting at the airport like ordinary people do. If they are so upset by your private jet, they should go and question the God who blessed your hustle and lifted you above your poor followers. Later, I will provide an in-depth explanation of how to fly private to the glory of God.

Bless women with your seed.

Some people may find it less than ideal to sleep with young female members of the congregation, but sometimes these things are beyond human comprehension. When you sleep with female members of the flock, do it with a level of grace that only the anointed can understand. Only God can judge you. And what is sin, when there is grace that abounds?

Ask people to sow seed.

(Because you have spread so much seed with the sisters in the church) ask people to sow seed so that God can bless them richly. Because if they do not sow seed by paying into the designated envelopes or bank accounts you have given them, nothing will grow in their lives and their souls and your finances will be as barren as dry shrubs out in the desert. They sow seed into your bank account, they get blessings, you get blessings, everybody is happy.

Do not pay tax.

Again, these many agents of the devil may spread rumours about your stupendous wealth and the luxury in which you live. Yes, you are making a profit, but whose business is that? Is it not where a person works that he will "eat"? Only wicked persons will want to deprive you of what they did not give to you. So what if your wealth is the result of weekly sermons about tithing? Humans, being what they are, will forget to give God his due. It is your duty to remind them, constantly. One of the problems is that people assume it is your money. You may be spending it, but it is not yours. You are only a caretaker. Those who assume that your taxes are useful for building infrastructure like roads and electricity, resources which you use a lot of, do not understand your relationship with God. People need to just calm down, pay their tithes, and trust you to know how to balance accounts with God.

Remind people to never, ever, speak evil against a man of God.

Like I said before, humans need reminding. Our rebellious nature sometimes gets the better of us and we begin to look too hard at the life of a man of God, or worry about his immorality. A man of God is not subject to the same rules as ordinary people. You have a level of grace that mere mortals cannot understand. You need to keep reminding your members to fear God and by extension, fear you. Because questioning you means questioning God. And all those who question you will not make heaven.

Hang out with politicians from time to time.

There is absolutely nothing wrong with you being close friends with government officials, even those who cannot provide the basic needs of citizens. There is nothing wrong with campaigning for them. And there is certainly nothing wrong with asking them to sow seed into your ministry when they come to visit. Was Jesus not a friend to harlots and tax collectors? And what on earth is worse than the reputation of tax collectors in the time of Jesus? You need to make corrupt people feel at ease in the presence of God; who knows, perchance they may be persuaded and accept the gospel of Jesus. Lay hands on them from time to time. And when they make huge donations, purify the money with the blood of Jesus and move on.

Nothing beats a good healing.

Claim to heal people from time to time. Sometimes you may have to hire and pay actors but it is all to draw people and make them believers. After all, did the Bible not say that God told Abraham to sacrifice his son when He knew he had a sheep waiting nearby? Was that not deception by human standards? But the scriptures say that the wisdom of the world is foolishness with God. While you perform miracles, however, never attempt to heal people who get injured in your church premises during say a stampede or the collapse of your church building. (Also, make predictions and prophecies about everything from politics to football but do not make predictions about your own life and church, even if a great tragedy is about to happen. This is bad karma. And sometimes God just prefers football to collapsing buildings. Don't ask me why. He works in mysterious ways).

Travel for crusades to perform signs and wonders with your personal physician.

You know how doctors are advised not to treat themselves or their family members? Well the same rule applies with men of God. No need to heal yourself or your family. After all, doctors also need to eat. And like Jesus, you like to feed multitudes.

How a wife supports her problematic but anointed husband.

When your wife, who is also a pastor in your church, catches you sleeping with other women and moves out of the house, ask your congregation to pray for her. Because it is your wife who needs the prayers, not you. It is her hard heart that needs healing and forgiveness so that she can recover from the mistake of exposing you and attempting to get a divorce. She does not realise what she will miss. Where else will she go to get seed as holy and anointed as yours?

Alternatively, make her do a video denying all allegations and giving an account of your faithfulness which people who try to make war against the kingdom of God refuse to see. Let her stand by you when you deny the allegations and call her mummy. The congregation will look into her eyes, see her certainty and know that there is no way you could have been involved in threesomes or ejaculating on the backs of strippers.

Use the word "da" in place of "the".

For example:

Da Lord wants you to give me his tithes for my private jet.

Da Bible says touch not my anointed.

Sounds nicer.

HOW TO FLY PRIVATE TO THE GLORY OF GOD

Being a pastor makes you different. Special. You are the manifestation of the spiritual in a temporal world. A pastor. The good Lord has blessed your glorious ministry. So, you find it unacceptable that you would be subjected to things like queuing for boarding passes, getting insulted by sinful plane passengers, arrival or departure delays. Especially the delays!

If people, those wicked critics, understood the spiritual implications of a delay, they wouldn't judge you. You are on your way to cast out a demon. Put anointing upon a child of God. Perform a crucial miracle. Attend to the vital matter of church expansion. A one-hour delay can make a demon wreak havoc on a child of God. It can indefinitely postpone an anointing or just annoy the spirit of God in you. You cannot afford to annoy the spirit of God and risk truncating your hustle. This is why you need a solution, a private jet.

It really doesn't matter whether you have one church in Bonny Island or a chain of churches larger than the Mr. Biggs fast food franchise. Flying private is crucial to the business of winning souls for the Lord.

First, being in the sky so close to heaven is not an experience you want to contaminate by letting someone who doesn't understand the will of God fly you. If you buy your own plane, you can choose your own pilot and even more importantly, your own passengers. Think of it: flying in the clouds, in the presence of the Almighty, surrounded by people with impure thoughts, people fleeing the will of God, adulterous people, crying babies interrupting your holy meditation. They even sell alcohol on some flights these days! You know how dangerous all of this can be. You remember in the Bible how Jonah, a disobedient child of God, nearly caused the shipwreck of a big ship. Only after Jonah was thrown out of that ship did the crew and passengers get respite from the angry waves. And with a plane, one cannot even throw out a sinner mid-flight from the sky without putting everyone on board in grave danger. If only people knew, they would understand: One sinner can jeopardise your safety.

To fly the plane, you need a godly pilot and co-pilot. True, the real pilot of your plane is no other than the Lord himself (or a designated angel), however you need human pilots to fill the seats. It is not enough that they went to aviation school or have flying experience. You would prefer a righteous born-again member of your church. But then not many of your church members can fit that role, so any born-again will do. You will not however hire someone from one of those atheist former countries of the Soviet Union or Eastern Europe. The pilots from there might be cheap and all, but no! No man that rejects God will fly your blessed plane.

The air hostesses will be chaste women who have never known a man biblically and will wear skirts to their ankles and blouses buttoned to the neck. Because to be in the bosom of the Lord is not a small matter. You don't want to annoy the Almighty. They can wear clothes sown with Ankara bearing imprints of Bible verses. They will sprinkle anointing oil during the flight. They will lead the flight in songs of praise and worship during take-off and landing, because these are the most dangerous periods of a flight. You will say the general prayer.

In fact, you are considering starting your own airline which will transport people in a godly way from one part of God's good earth to another. You play around with names in your head. "One With God Is Majority Airlines"— too long. "The Lord Is Good Airlines" — too common. "God's Time Airlines" — too ordinary. You think of "Blessed Wings Airlines" with the motto: Flying In The Bosom Of The Lord. Perfect.

Those people suggesting that because you can afford private jets you should suffer taxation, God will look into their matter and judge them appropriately. He also knows their number. They are enemies of your hustle. Have they not read that when one seeketh the kingdom every other thing shall be added to it? Do they expect God to give the earthly luxuries of this sinful world to sinners alone and not to you? Have they not read that with God all things are possible? Or maybe that is their problem — they cannot read. They cannot read the handwriting on the wall that this has come to stay. That your dominion has now reached the skies.

It doesn't matter that as you fly private, some members of your congregation walk 20 kilometres to church. As God takes care of the sparrow, so God will sort out their individual issues. It is your portion to fly private. Let no one wonder how you will pay to maintain the private jet, for the same God that blessed your hustle and arranged for a private jet will arrange for its maintenance. He is faithful.

May the good Lord whose blessing never fails meet you at the point of your needs and bless your hustle with a private jet.

IN SICKNESS AND IN HEALTH

HOW TO BE SICK

The Nigerian God is one of health and not of sickness. However, if you must be sick, here is how you must conduct yourself.

I know of European and American gods and goddesses who allow their worshippers to openly confess their illnesses to friends, neighbours and strangers. Sometimes they even go on TV shows and talk about what insidious viruses have attacked their bodies. There is a reason why we are happy and they are not. Our God does not approve of such shameful confessions. You must recognise as a worshipper that the body is a temple. Thus, confessing to a virus eating up your body in public is like saying that the owner of that temple cannot take care of his own house. God forbid that you should descend to such behaviour.

This however is not to deny the existence of viruses and bacteria which may from time to time pay visits to this temple. Far from it. But we must treat such events as what they are: mere temporary visitations from our less evolved relatives. Again, we know that one does not go proclaiming the details of a visitation from one's close relatives. Intimate things that happen during such visitations are to be kept within the family.

So, say you have been visited by a flu and you suffer headaches, running nose and weakness, you must, when asked, 'How are you?' reply, 'I am fine.' Conceal it until it becomes unbearable. Do not do rude things like refuse to shake people because you may transmit something contagious. Better a virus-ridden handshake than no handshake. Even when you sneeze without covering your mouth people will say with a smile, bless you.

The only exception to not talking about your own illness is when say you have malaria or a headache. Of course it is fine to talk about other people's illnesses and make suggestions regarding what we think is wrong with them.

If you harbour a treacherous virus like HIV you better not speak about it. We will ignore our personal lives and our own sexual behaviour and judge you for fornicating, for being a shameless sinner. It will not even matter if you did not get it from sexual intercourse. We will not care if it was from a blood transfusion, or through mother to child transmission. We just don't want you to mention it.

So, if you have lost a lot of weight and people begin to give you that look, you must quickly announce that your loss of weight is due to a visitation of a non-treacherous kind and then proceed to state in great detail what type of visitation it is. This will not stop Papa Chidera from asking Mama Bosede if she has seen how lean you have become lately. But it might prevent them from making the conclusion that you must have HIV. It will prevent them from drawing on history to back the claim — those nights they saw you with someone of the opposite sex and all the partners you have ever had. They may even try to help and offer prayers for your quick recovery.

There are no concerts to raise money for people with HIV. No short codes for people to SMS donations. No summoning God to take charge. Only stigma.

You may not be able to avoid illness. But you can avoid being judged for it.

HOW TO DIE

This is how to die in Nigeria.

1

You have to first of all understand that death is not a noun or a state. It is an event, the success of which requires proper planning.

2

One way to die is to ensure that in life, you did something worth remembering. This action need not be good or exemplary. In Nigeria no one cares if you were good or evil when you die. The only crime is dying without having done anything worthy of note. Like dying so poor no one knows your name. Death, especially that of someone rich or powerful, confers sainthood that cannot be challenged. Coup plotters and government thieves assume the title of elder statesmen and heroes of the nation. It will become forbidden to research your deeds and you will be beatified. You may even get a posthumous national award or have universities and streets named after you. And most importantly, the newspapers will carry ads about your unfortunate exit or "Call to Glory". In this way your death will have a meaning. So, please, to die in Nigeria, acquire power and wealth.

3

Do not die in the company of important people if you yourself have not attained importance or notoriety. If you go and die in the company of an ex-governor or ex-militant, the news will say Governor so-and-so has died in a ghastly motor accident. Then the report may add that "also among the casualties were two persons travelling in his convoy". No one will know which of the two unidentified persons you are. Or if you are male or female. You will pass on into oblivion without so much as an ad in the paper. Because in Nigeria, you are a number unless you are important. God forbid that this should happen to you.

The only exception to this is dying in a plane crash. This is the most respectable death for persons without a title to their name. The flight manifest — one of the few records that are consistently available on demand in Nigeria — makes it possible to have a full list of everyone on board. Usually this list is published and the world will receive notice of your untimely death. Your name will appear in full in newspapers and news reports. Your death will matter.

4

Do not make the mistake of dying in a luxury bus accident. You do not want to go out with the headline 'Dozens perish in bus crash'. Because to die is one thing and to perish is another. If you are unfortunate the reporter will say something like '25 crushed to death' with an emphasis on the crushing instead of the dying. All people will see in their heads will be human flesh being crushed. No face. No identity. No names.

5

Dying in a flood, a cholera outbreak, a collapsed building, these things are unacceptable. Rather than that, it is better to die while having carnal knowledge, in which case at least one of the tabloids or gossip blogs will find out your name and carry your story. Your family may not like it, but at least people will know your name.

6

One of the worst places to die however is in a terrorist attack. Nigeria is not one of those countries where they respectfully identify dead people by name. When a terrorist kills you here, whether as a student in a school or a traveller on the road, you are summarised into a number or fraction. An official of the National Emergency Management Agency (NEMA) was once quoted as saying that when fatalities occur in a conflict situation, they feel duty bound to reduce the figures, so as not to escalate the crises. What wise thinking. So, if there are 200 deaths, NEMA may report 60. Or just cancel one zero and say 20. Imagine being summarised. Not even counted as a whole dead figure. So, if you run into a terrorist bent on taking your life, beg the man. Tell him you are not opposed to dying for his cause. Plead with him to try something else, maybe make a video or something. Because it would be a tragedy to fade into oblivion, unannounced.

7

One great way to go is to die on camera. Hundreds, including school children, may die or be slaughtered every month in Maiduguri and Nigerians will go about their daily activities. Maiduguri is just one faraway North Eastern state that could pass for a territory of Chad or Niger Republic. In their heads 160 killed in Borno is what it is, a number. But if you have your death captured on tape, perfect. Then you can have NGOs calling for legislation to outlaw whatever type of knife they used to stab you. If you are fortunate, your name will trend on Twitter and hashtags will spring up like #MakeSicklesIllegal, #VictorSickleSlaughter, #OutlawSickleStabbingNOW, #Justice4Tolu, #NeverAgain or #R.I.P.Kevin. People will grant interviews and there will be hundreds of badly written blogs about you. And believe me, a hashtag and a badly written blog post with a link to your death video or a photo of you gotten from Facebook is better than dying as a number. The only exception to this is dying as a hated minority. Like a Shiite. Or a Biafra protester. If you die while hated, whether on camera or not, we will spit on your grave. Just don't be a minority. Or if you cannot help it, then try the best you can to avoid dying. May an untimely death not befall you, but if it does, may it be sexy enough for a hashtag.

You cannot leave your death to chance. Because, to die is human but to die properly is divine.

TEMPORAL

HOW TO SHOW LOVE

This is how to show Nigerian love.

Our love is not of short-lived flowers and long meaningless walks in the park. Nigerian love is pragmatic. Words are a waste of time. Every true Nigerian knows how little the words "I love you" mean. Except of course if you are in Europe and need to quickly marry someone to get residency. When you hear rich couples attend events and say those nebulous words, "I love you" to each other, what they do not tell you is how they really say it. God will judge them for trying to mislead new couples.

Nigerian love is a very material concept. Cook for your man. Nigerian wives know this already. But lovers need to learn: a thousand words cannot work the magic of one pot of egusi soup complete with meat, "assorted" and okporoko. Present it steaming with semovita or if you can, pounded yam. You will not need to say anything. He will wear a smile that says "I know you love me". His friends, on learning that the wondrous dish was made by you, will proclaim, 'O boy! Dis girl like you well-well o'. In Nigerian pidgin, to like "well-well" is to love practically and "o" as an intensifier for "well-well" has no real English equivalent — the closest to it would be, love to a superlative degree.

Cooking for him entitles you to show your love in another very important way: checking his phone. You have cooked for him and he has shown his gratitude by sweating profusely and promptly falling asleep on your couch. This is the time to dive for his phone and read all his text messages. You will find something. If you don't, go through his call records — you are likely to find calls to or from an Amaka after he said he needed to rest last night. Whether you choose to further show your love by harassing him about it immediately, or choose to hold onto it as part of your arsenal during your next big quarrel is up to you. You know what works best for your man.

Loving Nigerian men always pay. There is no exception to this rule. Not even if she has watched plenty foreign shows on DSTV and pretends that she wants to split the bill. If a Nigerian girl offers to pay reject it like Jesus rejected Satan's evil temptation with bread. Don't even act like it is a discussion. Ignore her attempts at checking her purse and just settle the bill. This is true love. This also applies if she is out with one, two or three friends. Whether you choose to show your love quietly, by excusing yourself and going to settle the enormous bill, or with panache, by screaming, 'How much is MY bill?' is up to you. You know what works best for your woman.

As a loving Nigerian woman, never ask who his female friends are. Even if you find him in a compromising situation with a woman who refuses to greet you. Nigerian love ignores such things. It makes excuses on his behalf — she may be his colleague, business partner or member of his prayer group. Nigerian love is good like that. This doesn't however mean that you can do the same. Nigerian love has very gender specific rules. They do not apply both ways. The only exception to this rule is if the Nigerian man does not "pay".

Deny her the company of any male who is not her relative. This is important. In Nigeria, a jealous man is a loving man. If she is on the phone, watch her demeanour. If she is excited, ask her who it is. By "who?" you mean all the details — name, gender, nature of relationship, process and length of acquaintance, subject of conversation, the whole works. She knows this. You own the franchise of her happiness and no other man is allowed to make her laugh. If you fail to do this, even she will begin to doubt your love. You cannot afford to let this to happen.

Never ever as a Nigerian man do stupid things like go into the kitchen to cook. This is forbidden territory. Not even if you are starving and she is on the bed complaining of cramps. There is no better way to truncate your romantic hustle than doing the dishes after she has spent hours making your favourite dish. This is like jumping into a river with a concrete slab tied to your neck. There is no recovery from it. God will judge all the foreign film makers who have introduced the dangerous illusion of this being a romantic thing. In fact, when you answer the door and it is your neighbour asking if you have a baking tin or big pot, deny knowledge of anything that goes on in the kitchen and ask her to hold on for your woman. It will be a tragedy for you to introduce doubts about your masculinity in your woman's mind. May God protect us from tragedies.

It is my hope that as you enjoy foreign romance movies or romance novels, you do not get carried away by them. Stick to my advice and God will bless your romantic hustle.

HOW TO OWN A SLAVE

The Nigerian God is faithful. He has blessed your hustle with a husband. With a God-fearing wife. We give him all the praise.

As a Nigerian husband, your wife needs assistance. Look away and provide it. Do not ask too many questions. You work as a team. If you hear the girl screaming do not intervene. Now step aside while I tell your wife how to do this properly.

As a Nigerian wife, you began your wifely hustle by going out of your way to show your dutifulness, things that would make him go online and thank God for blessing him thus — cooking, cleaning and never saying no to him. God will meet you at the point of your needs and bless you for this. However, something is happening to you. Tiredness is setting in. You feel nauseous and irritated. The doctor has told you that you are having a baby. You and your husband agree that you cannot keep up with the housework with this growing human mass in your tummy. It is time for a house help. Your husband has left you to take care of it.

You have many choices. There is the choice of young poor girls from the North who have been trained to work like horses, want little and show gratitude for whatever they receive. The girl may have thinning brown hair from lack of nutrition and may look stunted at 12 but trust me, she knows how to fetch water, wash piles of clothes and sweep endlessly.

You also have the choice of taking in the pre-pubescent out-of-wedlock daughter of that distant cousin whom you have never met in your village. You had heard that a boy got her pregnant at 14 and ran away thereafter. Since then the daughter has suffered stigma and neglect that has blocked any chances of your cousin getting a husband. Those village people can be unforgiving.

There is that aunt in the village who promised you someone to help when you came for your traditional marriage. You turned down the offer then. Now is the time to call that aunt and tell her that the housework will kill you soon. She will laugh on the other end of the line and tell you not to worry. You will remind her that you don't want a boy o! Boys are hard to control. 'I have heard,' she will say and in one or two weeks you will receive your package of an awkward prepubescent girl.

Then there is the international connection — the kids from Togo or Benin Republic. Someone has told you of these young kids from Benin Republic whose salary you will pay to a man who will claim to be their uncle or cousin. Hard working children with nowhere to go. Nowhere to run. Perfect.

Let me just say clearly that you do not need a person of legal age, an adult who will one day kill you all in your sleep, kidnap or bewitch your children or worse, (and God forbid) snatch your husband from you. Don't roll your eyes and say your husband would never do that. We all know how men are trash. You need a child. Anyone who quotes the Child's Right Act and calls employing anyone under the legal age child labour, God will give them paralysis of the mouth. How else do they want you to get the housework done without arousing your poor husband?

When the young girl comes, the first thing to do is to, without her consent, test her for hepatitis, HIV and other infections. You don't want her bringing diseases into your godly, healthy home. If you must, go to the second-hand store and buy her two old dresses — one for work and one for sleep. Or maybe one extra for church, which you must warn her only to wear on Sundays. You can't have her embarrassing you too much in church. If you don't have boys' quarters, clear out the store so she can sleep there. Otherwise get an old mattress that she will use somewhere in a corner of the living room. As she is the first to wake and last to sleep, you won't have to see it at all so don't worry.

You need to cut her hair. It is better. Both of you should not be struggling to groom your hair. You can't have her stealing your expensive hair products. Anything a small comb or brush can't do must go. The more unattractive she looks, the better for you and your marriage. Like I said before, it is not your fault that men are trash. Design flaw.

There is no need to waste money sending her to school. It is not your fault that her parents can't afford to. In fact, she should be grateful that you are giving her a rare opportunity to come to the city and make some money. If she spends all her time at school, when will she do the housework? But if you absolutely have to, find a cheap school, maybe one with evening classes she can attend. Something simple that won't confuse her about her station in life. Imagine taking her to a place where she learns about discombobulating ideas like human rights. God forbid!

Discipline: Very important. Sometimes screaming degrading insults is not enough to put an ungrateful, sloppy house help in line. The phrase "spare the rod and spoil the child" includes the children who do your household chores and care for your family. Sometimes they get too comfortable. Sometimes they are possessed by demons. Only a healthy dose of flogging, chaining and starvation can rid them of evil spirits or too much comfort.

Watch the food she eats. Especially the meat. Nothing makes a house help grow wings like pieces of meat. Meat has a way of creating a sense of entitlement in a person. Especially chicken. You don't want that to happen.

Don't make the mistake of allowing her to have friends. Whether with the help next door or with the one in the shop down the street or the one grinding tomatoes near the market. She did not come to your house to play and network. Next thing you know they will connive and do something evil to you.

Sometimes, no matter how hard you try, there comes a time when you must let the house help go. Such instances include when you notice that she has become a woman and is almost needing the same bra size as you. Like I said three million times, men are what? Men are trash! They see breasts and they lose their minds. You need to be proactive and protect your husband from himself. Send her away and look for another prepubescent one to take her place.

Do not go looking for answers where you have no business looking. If the man who brought a girl from Benin Republic says he is her Uncle, then he is her Uncle. If he says he will hold her salary for her, then he will. The less you know the better. Giving money to a third party ensures that it will be safe.

Do these and the wonderful Nigerian God will, through your enslaved person, lighten your load and bless your hustle.

So, Nigerian husband, like I said before, don't ask. As long as your children are being taken care of and the food is on the table and the house is clean, then everything is as God planned it to be. God bless!

HOW TO COMMUNICATE IN TIMES OF CRISES

To create is divine and to destroy is human. You did not cause this. You are aware that the history of humans is the history of crisis. Your country is no exception. As a politician, there is no need to be unusually perturbed when there is a crisis in the county. This is the way of the world. And a country without this is a boring country. Who wants to be uneventful like Norway or Finland?

As a government official this is how you must conduct yourself when you suddenly hear that Christians and Muslims have started killing each other.

One thing you must be careful with is truth. Truth is like a double-edged knife. Sometimes it can be an impressive tool for cutting things into precise shapes, other times it can be a mean tool of destruction or even a self-destructive thing, hurting the bearer beyond expectation. You must be careful who you give truth to. Not everyone deserves it or can use it. Withhold it for as long as you can. Sometimes the flip side of the truth is not a lie, but only useful, responsible silence. So when a journalist comes asking questions during a crisis, you must treat them with suspicion for you cannot be certain whose agents they are. Many a journalist is an unwitting agent of the enemy. You give them truth and they stab you with it. You must try as much as possible not to respond to official inquiries for information whether brought pursuant to the

Freedom of Information Act or any similar law that is subject to abuse by journalists. You must never feel guilty about this. It is the same as refusing to give a toddler a knife to play with. The toddler will cry and stomp its feet. But you know you are doing right by that toddler.

Especially when there is violent conflict, you must never, ever, provide accurate figures of those who have died. The reason is simple: You do not want anybody getting angry and threatening or carrying out reprisals. As much as you can control it, you must prevent journalists from taking pictures at the scene.

It is important to claim that all is well. The good book says death and life are in the power of the tongue. I will add that peace and conflict are in the power of a press release. Unless you have had to impose a curfew, you must use phrases like, "normalcy is fast returning", and "people are going about their normal activities".

Being a reporter during a time of crisis can be confusing. My rule has always been, when in doubt say the opposite of what the government says. It is sufficient to make a few calls after which you can publish unverified information. There is that phrase that cures all known defects in a report and you must learn how to use it: "All attempts to reach so-and-so for comment proved abortive."

When people make inflammatory statements, you must never apply too much scrutiny to it. You are a journalist, not their mother or a man of God. Your job is just to report. Sometimes you will hear of journalists in a crisis situation being selective and choosing not to report certain things. God forbid that you play God. You are a messenger and a messenger is not concerned about the contents of the envelope, only that the envelope reaches its intended destination. A typical example of what you must avoid is how some journalists covered the crises between the IRA and the British government. Some of them decided not to report every single bombing that took place especially when there was no casualty. And what excuse did they give for such irresponsibility? That terrorism is all about spreading terror and that they would not report every single attempt at creating such terror. How presumptuous! May such bad behaviour never be mentioned about you.

Report every case of bombings, even the failed attempts. People need to know all the activities of the terrorists. Let them choose which one affects them. If a bag was found abandoned in a public building and there is a bomb threat which turns out to be innocuous, you are allowed to use bold headlines like "Bomb Scare in Ikeja". You are reporting it as it is, and that is what a good journalist should be: accurate.

There is no need to work alongside government when there is an outbreak of violence. If you wanted to be involved in the politics of things, you would have contested for office.

Very importantly however, life is for the living. Leave real-time conflict reporting to foreign journalists. It is wrong to want to actually cover a violent crisis or war. That is what phones and texts and emails are for, even though sometimes the government may cut off phone lines in the area. Taking the next flight or bus to Maiduguri, whether as an embedded journalist with soldiers or otherwise, is not journalism. It is foolishness. People should be patient, they will hear about it after the fighting is over.

Where there is an explosion do not fail to suggest that it might be a bomb. The facts might be hazy but it is important for people to know that they might be dealing with a bomb there.

Where there is an explosion you can help a militant group like Boko Haram take responsibility by writing in such a way that suggests it had to be them. The rule is simple: report first, verify later. It is not your fault that government won't respond quickly with the right information.

To spice it all up, never forget to splash photos of the bodies of victims and wounded people in your paper because as they say, a picture is worth more than a thousand reports.

And you, the blessed NGO, whom God has elevated to the position of saviour of your brothers, have a special place in all of this. You must be on your toes, ready to publish a press release when there seems to be any case of human rights violation or whatever other type of violation you have told your funders you will monitor. It may not always be necessary to thoroughly examine the event that has just occurred. You don't want your funders to think you are sloppy, being the last to condemn a thing. Do not fail to use the words "condemn in the strongest terms". Do not fail to make a demand. For someone's resignation or unconditional release. Your funders will be happy.

As a Christian or Muslim organisation, your role in a time of crisis is really simple. You must remember your calling and the people you represent. When violent crisis breaks out with members of another religion, you must begin by claiming that your people suffered more casualties and that you will not accept this. Do not mention members of the other religion who died. They do not matter. They may not even make heaven. Say that you will no longer fold your arms and watch these criminal killings continue. Add that if the government doesn't immediately do something, you may be forced to look for your own solutions. Where possible, circulate videos and photos of the bodies of your brethren who were slaughtered by members of the other religion. Do not talk about any reprisals your own people have carried out.

Communication is important during a crisis. With these tips, together, whether as government, journalists, NGOs or faith based organisations, I am sure that we can succeed, and that God, seeing our hearts, will bless our hustle.

HOW TO CONDUCT A MEETING

A Nigerian meeting is not just an event. It is that sacred, multipurpose, indispensable tool for living the Nigerian life. This is how to conduct a Nigerian meeting.

1

As a business owner, always call for meetings even for things you can do by email. Sometimes, meet early in the morning for morning devotion to commit your business and hustle to the hands of God. Meet to set the agenda for other meetings that will be held over the week. Meet to review previous meetings.

Jobs are boring. You need a distraction. Meetings, especially ones with tea breaks, prevent you from losing your mind and picking up a gun to shoot all your annoying colleagues like white people do. White people need to have more meetings.

When going for a meeting, never arrive early. This will give the impression that you are jobless, desperate or too eager. Nobody likes Nigerians who are jobless or too eager. A true Nigerian — not one who is pretending to be white — will understand if you show up late for a meeting. They may feign annoyance, but usually they will wait. In fact, the best of Nigerians will make excuses for you, especially if you live in a place like Lagos. You will walk in late to a meeting, panting, with that faux look of contrition and the person you are having a meeting with — if she is a good Nigerian — will say: 'Eiyah! Traffic abi?' You will only have to nod or say something like:

'No be small tin o.' Everyone will be grateful that you showed up and the meeting will begin.

When you are having a big meeting with an "oga", or an "oga-madam" it is safer to cancel all other appointments for the day. Because the oga will saunter in three hours late and you will have to smile and say 'No, not at all!' when she asks: 'Did I keep you waiting?'

2

If you are an oga, you should never, ever show up for a meeting on time. This is Nigeria. People disrespect ogas who don't keep them waiting forever. They will think you are equals and before you know it one ordinary person will call your name without adding Chief or Chief Mrs or Prof or Honorable or Distinguished or Your Excellency. God forbid that after hustling to get those titles, some idiot forgets to mention them. All because you came early to a meeting.

3

As a proper Nigerian whose father is God, you must commit all meetings to His hands. You may work hard but it is God that is in charge of blessing your hustle. Never forget to say at least two prayers in every meeting. One Christian, one Muslim. You never know which of the Gods will answer favourably. It does not matter if you will be discussing how to steal from other people. God sees the heart and he knows that deep down, all you want to do is succeed. And God helps those who help themselves.

4

When it is your turn to speak at a meeting it is rude to go straight to the point. Proper Nigerians are not rude. Below is a summary of how to speak at a Nigerian meeting:

a. Don't be ungrateful. Thank the moderator for giving you the opportunity to speak. Begin by saying, "I want to take this opportunity to thank..."

b. Don't be disrespectful. Observe all protocol. People did not become highly placed by mistake. You think becoming Chief or Chief (Mrs.) is a joke?

c. Show appreciation. Say how much it is a privilege for you to be at the meeting. Use the phrases "singular honour" and "rare privilege".

d. Show understanding. Explain how important the meeting is to you and to everyone present. Thank the conveners for having the wisdom to organise the meeting.

e. Show regard for the last speaker. Use words like "just like the last speaker has said" or "I want to concur with the last speaker" or "I totally agree with the last speaker" or "I want to align myself with the last speaker". Then proceed to say the same thing using your own words. It is important for everyone to have a chance to speak at a meeting.

f. Be considerate. Promise not to speak too long with a phrase like: "I will not take much of your time", after which you can speak freely.

g. Always provide a summary of all you have just said. Use phrases like: "So, what have I just said?" or "What am I trying to say?" to introduce your summary.

h. Be observant. If you still have more things to say and you sense that people are tired of hearing you speak, use the words

"In conclusion" to give them hope that you will soon end, after which you can continue to speak freely. Hope is a great thing.

5

All meetings must end in a closing prayer. To avoid a fight however, take care to remember whether it was a Christian prayer or Muslim prayer you began with. When you are not sure, do both prayers. You do not want to annoy any children of the Nigerian God.

6

One last thing: Don't forget that the only acceptable way of answering a phone call during a Nigerian meeting is to shout: "Hello, please I am in a meeting, let me call you back." People will smile, seeing how important this meeting is to you.

I hope that this helps and that God will continue to bless your hustle as you conduct meetings.

HOW TO BE A CAR OWNER

You have crossed that awkward, deeply uncomfortable, sometimes shameful, social state of being without a car. I mean, in some countries where the public transport system works, not having a car is no big deal. But you are in Nigeria, where public transport is living hell, and owning a car can be the difference between life and social death.

You had suffered the humiliation and attendant frustrations. You swore to yourself, after the girl you came to a party with left in an air-conditioned car, that things must change. The Nigerian God felt your pain, heard your cries of affliction and consequently, after much tithing and prayers, blessed your hustle. Enough to buy your own car. I rejoice with you.

You have taken the car to the man of God and they have spent over an hour with the bonnet open, anointing your car and protecting it against the spirit of accidents that those jealous neighbours and village enemies are sure to send your way. That is fine. But you also need my advice.

Your car is not beautiful unless you have covered it in stickers. Get one from your church or fellowship that declares this year to be your "year of anointing", or your "year of unsurpassed success". If your wife or husband goes to a different church, get one from there too. You can never get too many. Get one sticker that declares your child to be a Star Student. Let those with dull children see it and regret that their wives didn't take enough vitamins during pregnancy. Because of police on the road, get either a Nigerian Bar Association sticker or an Army sticker. You don't have to be a lawyer or soldier to get them. Especially the NBA one — you can find that one in any court premises for one or two hundred Naira.

Depending on how much God has blessed your hustle, get a customised plate number with your name or nickname, such as TONY01; DE DON 01; DADDY K. The '01' is useful even if you have only one car. It just shows how much faith you have that more will come. Otherwise, depending on your level of gratitude to God, you can use a nice Bible verse, like ISAIAH43:4 so that people can know how precious you are in His eyes.

Now that you are a car owner, you need to realise that your status has changed. You need to treat pedestrians with the disdain they deserve. It doesn't matter that you were once a pedestrian crossing these same streets. You must never think like a pedestrian and do silly things like observing zebra crossings. Those white lines are there to beautify the road. Speed across them and curse anyone who tries to get in your way.

Your neighbours need to feel your presence. They need to see just how your hustle has been blessed. Every morning, remind them by "warming" your car. This process involves waking up at 6 a.m. and revving your car engine loudly until the neighbours wake up to the evidence of your blessed hustle.

You bought the car with your hard-earned cash. And that includes the car horns. Those who call your right to honk noise pollution, God will judge them appropriately and truncate their hustle. In fact, if you ask me, because of how important it is, your right to use your horn indiscriminately should be constitutionally guaranteed. Honk in the morning when your wife is wasting your time inside and you need her to hurry up. Honk when you see your neighbours. Honk in a traffic jam even though you are sure this will not make the cars miraculously move. Honk instead of slowing down when you are approaching a junction or intersection. Honk when you are angry. And when you are happy. There are few things as useful in a car as the horn.

At night, it is important that you see the road clearly. Nigerian roads are dark and dangerous, so you must use your full lights at all times. It doesn't matter if you are blinding oncoming vehicles. Is it your fault that the government is not doing their job?

Other things you will learn on the job as a car owner include how to double park, how to drive against traffic on the highway, how to create multiple lanes in a traffic jam, how to beat traffic lights, how to stop in the middle of the road to say hello to a long lost friend, how to litter the street with wrappers of plantain chips bought in a hold-up, all of which every true and experienced Nigerian driver is adept at doing. I trust you will catch up quickly.

Once again I rejoice with you and may God keep blessing your hustle.

WORKING PEOPLE, WORKING HARD

HOW TO USE A BUSINESS CARD

The word "business" is a cliché, the relevance of which has attained gargantuan proportions in Nigeria. Business meetings — anything from seeing an ex-girlfriend that one has sworn to his current girlfriend or wife that he is not sleeping with, to paying your carpenter for the side stool he fixed — are sacred. Business partners typically have the most intense form of relationship. "Businessman" or "Businesswoman" is the nebulously omnibus job description that solves the problem of having to explain why one is idle or why one has so much money without any visible or legal source of income. Being "into business" can mean anything from importing cheap substandard goods from China to having a rich generous lover. Some statistics say that the majority of Nigerians are into agriculture. That is a blatant lie. The majority of Nigerians are into "business". Now, you may be forgiven if you don't have an actual business in Nigeria. But it is a mortal sin not to have a business card, otherwise known as complimentary card or just card.

It goes beyond sinning to not have a business card. It is an existential issue of the highest degree. It questions your identity as a Nigerian. Recently I have been going about my normal business, pun intended, without a business card. When I say I don't want children, people greet me with surprise. But when I say I have no business card (not that I have run out of cards) they greet me with horror. I get the you-are-an-evil-alien-that-deserves-to-die look. That look isn't nice. You don't want to lie in bed wondering why bad things happen to good people. To avoid this, you must understand the business of business cards.

Whether you are a "General Contractor" or "Friend of His Excellency the Executive Governor", the business card can prove to be more important than the business. Consequently, you must take care in its production. A floppy, dull-looking card can be an instant business death sentence. Your card precedes you. Many times that will be the only contact you will make. Make it nice, firm, glossy. Or gold-embossed if you have anything to do with His Excellency, the President or His Excellency, the Executive Governor

Make sure you have at least three phone numbers on the card. This shows you have at least three phones. No self-respecting business Nigerian takes this for granted. True, one of the phones may be a cheap China dual-sim phone but nobody can tell — three numbers show you don't muck around with your business. It is not your fault that not a single network provider in Nigeria can be relied upon. Whoever criticises your three phones, may their own businesses collapse.

You need titles. Every academic qualification must be clearly printed. If you are a lawyer for example it is not enough to write your name and call yourself a legal practitioner. That is a waste of space on a business card. You need to add Barrister in front of your name and Esq behind. Then you must add LLB (Hons), BL and any other acronym you have acquired including all those management and arbitration courses they advertised to you in Law School and during NYSC. Below all of this you will write out your full title: Barrister and Solicitor of the Supreme Court of the Federal Republic of Nigeria. Only another bad-belle lawyer can fail to see the significance of all of this.

You must keep your business cards handy. You never know when you will run into someone rich, famous or extremely beautiful who has no time to wait for you to search your six pockets and fat multi-layered wallet for your business card. Get a nice card holder. Or arrange them nicely in your breast pocket.

Striking up a conversation using business cards is an art that takes you everywhere from doing business to someone's bed. Meet a total stranger on a plane and as you look into their eyes, put your hand in your breast pocket and slide out your business card in time to coincide with 'Hi, my name is Emeka. But you can call me Mekus.' It will not matter if you are as useless to each other as a condom to an impotent man. A proper introduction is all that counts. They will take your business card and stare into it pretending to care, by which time you will have gotten their attention. The rest, if you are smart, will become history.

May the good God who guides all things Nigerian, guide you and your business cards to people who will bless your hustle.

HOW TO IDENTIFY A MIDDLE-CLASS NIGERIAN

I believe it is time to conclusively tackle the question: who is a member of the Nigerian middle class? There are several definitions of "middle class", many not valid for our peculiar context. Also, I don't like all that jargon that economists use. I have therefore decided to explain what this thing called middle class is in Nigeria and which persons would fall into this category. Forget what foreign economists say. This is the real deal.

The generator

In Nigeria, a person who is able to purchase a generator for personal use and run said generator every time power goes off is a member of the middle class. Note that this is different from the group of lower-class people who are able to save to buy generators for their small-scale business like hair salons or barber shops. Middle class people own a generator at home.

In this category, lower middle class will be people whose generator cannot power all the appliances in the house and who have to make crucial decisions like whether they will use the refrigerator or the air conditioner. Not both. The upper middle class are those whose generators can carry all the appliances they own and who don't have to worry about the refrigerator being off when the generator is being turned on. So, in a lower middle-class house, you will likely hear someone screaming as they try to turn on the noisy generator: 'Una don off evrytin?'

Phone credit

Mobile telephony is big in Nigeria. Often however, many in the lower classes have need to say that their "credit" ran out. Sometimes they send those "Please Call Me" messages. God forbid that a middle-class Nigerian threatens their standing in life and society by sending a "Please Call Me" message. Members of this class are those who never have to tell you "I could have called you but I don't have credit." They can afford to top up as soon as their credit runs out.

In this category, lower middle class are those who can afford to top up almost immediately but sometimes have to tell the people they are calling: 'Please let me go across the road to buy recharge card, I will call you back.' (Or better still, 'Hold on, let me send my house-girl to buy me credit.') I know many lower class people use this "I will call you back" line too. But the difference between a lower-class person and a (lower) middle-class person is that the middle-class person often does go and buy the credit. The middle-class person calls you back.

The upper-middle-class person in this category is one who never runs out of credit, because they top up regularly without waiting for it to finish. That is the main difference: lower-middle-class wait until their credit finishes before running out to buy credit (or using a short code to top up) while the upper middle class doesn't need a reason to top up — they are just cool like that.

The cinema

I know that we don't have a big cinema culture, but at least in our major cities, this is one way to know persons who are in the middle class. Middle-class Nigerians can afford movie tickets, often for themselves and their families and/or lovers as frequently as (once or more) every week. While movies tickets are not completely out of reach for lower-class people, what differentiates the middle class from others is not only the frequency with which they can go but also the crucial fact that they can afford the overpriced popcorn that is traditionally part of the cinema experience and don't need to smuggle home cooked food into the cinema. While lower-class people can save and go to the cinema on special occasions like Eid, Easter or Christmas, the middle-class person doesn't need a special occasion to go to the cinema. In this category, the upper-middle-class people actually avoid the cinema on public holidays so as to avoid mixing with the lower-class people who have saved to enjoy this experience. You can't be mixing with lower-class people. God did not elevate you for nothing.

The car

A middle-class Nigerian owns a car. If they do not have a car it is usually because they are saving to buy a really fancy car and would rather take taxis than go through the stress of driving a problematic second-hand Japanese car. However, some lower-class people happen upon some cash and buy cars — like those who are able to save and buy taxis or cars which they use for work, like Uber. There are cars and there are cars.

While a lower-class person will often abandon their car as soon as fuel scarcity bites hard, the middle-class person is often able, albeit through much complaining, to buy very expensive fuel from the black market to keep their car running. During periods of fuel scarcity also, the difference between the upper and lower middle class becomes clear. The upper-middle-class person will experience no change in driving habits while the lower-middle-class person will do things like stop using the air conditioner or turn off the engine in traffic or when they stop at traffic lights. On social networking sites like Twitter for example, you will find lower-middle-class people tweeting about their fuel woes and how much they bought a gallon for. Or they will shamelessly put out an SOS asking who knows where they can get fuel. Upper-middle-class people never do shameful things like tweet photos of their fuel tank during fuel scarcity or celebrate when they find fuel. This is because (a) the upper-middle-class god is faithful (b) they are usually connected to someone who can provide them fuel and never have to queue themselves and (c) they are afraid that if they confess that they do have fuel, their lower-middle-class friends will beg them for some. And there are many people in this lower middle class. You help one, they go and brag to all their friends and you find a dozen strangers begging you for fuel. Because yes, no one brags like lower-middle-class people. To avoid this kind of situation, it is not uncommon for upper-middle-class people to become hypocrites: join the rest of Nigeria in complaining about the fuel situation without providing any specifics. In war, you must practice diversion and deception. The class warfare in Nigeria is real.

DSTV

Cable television is an important aspect of middle-class life in Nigeria. DSTV is one defining characteristic of Nigeria's middle class. Again, sometimes, a person from the lower class may happen upon some money and buy a DSTV satellite dish and decoder. But often the lower-class person will go some months without a valid subscription. A middle-class person always has a valid subscription and even when DSTV increases their charges, they will complain and create hashtags to protest the increase, but go ahead and pay. Because they cannot live without DSTV. The difference here between the upper and lower middle class is that the upper-middle-class person will never complain about subscriptions and will always have the premium bouquet. The lower-middle-class person changes bouquets depending on their finances. And they always, always complain.

Connections

Many Nigerians try to better their lives, but often, in the absence of real power, they leave matters to God. The middle class, while still cherishing the immense power of God, know the truth in the saying: God helps those who help themselves.

A middle-class Nigerian is one who knows a person in government or authority who can change the course of events in their favour. It can be admission into university for their children, the fast tracking of an application or other processes, or even buying bread which is in high demand from a crowded supermarket. A middle-class person prays first and then looks for someone who can write them a note that can work wonders. Because God works through mysterious middlemen. What differentiates the upper-middle-class Nigerian from the lower middle class are the degrees of separation between them and the person(s) with real power. So, for example, while a lower-middle-class person may have to go to their uncle who knows an ex-local government chairman who knows one of the members of the governing council of a university who can speak to the vice chancellor for their child's admission, an upper-middle-class person may have been classmates with the Governor's wife and can beg her directly to include their child's name on the list the Governor sends to the Vice Chancellor for admission.

International travel

Nigerians of all social classes love to travel. Yes, they may all be travelling for different reasons, but they all at least try to travel. While many in the lower class may not be able to afford to travel or meet visa requirements, a few do, either smuggling their way to Europe and finding a way to stay illegally or taking the dangerous trip by sea or desert. Middle-class Nigerians, however, take pride in their travels. They invest in their travels. They talk about where they have been and show off items they bought from abroad.

In this category, one difference between the lower and upper-middle-class Nigerian is that the lower-middle-class Nigerian is more noisy about their travels, from the visa application process to talking about the bags and shoes they bought in Dubai. For every visa a lower-middle-class person has, they have applied for four. They are relentless and throw dignity to the wind until they get the visa they need to travel. If they couldn't get the US or UK visa, they will try Malaysia. If they don't get that, they will try Dubai or South Africa. And they will keep coming back until the US or UK sees the dozen Asian visas on their passport and gives them that visa. Often, a conversation between two lower-middle-class persons will consist of sharing tales about visa application or asking each other what visas they have and how long it took to finally get them. A visa is life for the lower-middle-class Nigerian. An upper-middle-class Nigerian however, might have already schooled abroad. Yes, maybe in Cyprus or Ukraine, but to most Nigerians schooling abroad is schooling abroad. So they have gotten the visa panic out of their system. They travel noiselessly and probably post pictures of their vacations just so their friends can keep up with them. The lower-middle-class Nigerian will turn on their internet location as soon as they leave the plane so that no one on Twitter or Facebook will doubt their travels or their middle-class status. No one fears losing their status like the lower-middle-class Nigerian. No one brags like the lower-middle-class Nigerian.

Lower-middle-class Nigerian conversations are peppered with phrases like:

"When I was in London (or Hoostun Tehzahs or Atlanta or Dubai or Tchicago or Europe...)"

"That's not how they do it in London (or Hoostun Tehzahs or Atlanta or Dubai or Tchicago or Europe...)"

I could go on and on. If you belong to one of these categories and have not previously considered yourself a middle-class Nigerian because of some silly criteria from some foreign economist, I urge you to claim it. Claim it and celebrate it. And if you are in the lower-middle-class, I pray that God blesses you and lifts you into the upper-middle-class. Because, trust me, there is nothing that the Nigerian God cannot do. He can make one of your friends get into power and help you get contracts that will instantly take you from a used Honda to a brand-new Kia or Hyundai. And from that point to real riches, it is only a matter of time, greed, connections and loyalty. God bless your hustle.

P.S. I know this is difficult, but if God does bless your hustle and you move from lower to upper middle class, try, try to respect yourself and leave lower-middle-class behaviour behind. Like bragging. Or talking about your visas. Or how many times you went for "summer". Or how they do it in London (or Hoostun Tehzahs or Atlanta or Dubai or Tchicago or Europe...).

P.P.S. I know it seems like I have bad mouthed lower-middle-class people. But here is one great side of the lower-middle-class Nigerian: they are the most generous. Perhaps because of fear of becoming poor or desperation to reach upper middle class, the lower-middle-class person regularly gives money to beggars, especially those who beg in God's name. They tithe regularly. They will not risk losing any chance to have their hustle blessed by God. Every donation is an investment in securing their position in the middle class and possibly bettering it.

God bless lower-middle-class people.

HOW TO BE A MECHANIC

Life is nothing without you. People may run away from you, despise you, but in their hearts they know, they need you. You are the one who saves the day: the woman stranded with an overheated car in a hold up, the lover whose car threatens to truncate his hustle, the transporter who needs his cars back on the road to make money. You get the desperate calls, you see their worried faces. You arrive and gaze like a prophet into the engine. You spend more time than it actually takes, but you get it done. Like magic, the car comes back to life. People don't think about you unless they are in trouble. I am here to give you the prominence you deserve and teach those who intend to learn the trade just what they must do.

You need to appear dirty. A mechanic gains nothing by having presentable work clothes. How else will the car owner know you have worked on his car if he doesn't have grease stains on his seats, steering wheel, dashboard, everywhere?

As a mechanic, you must prefer women. Not the restless, jobless ones who pretend to be men and try to truncate your hustle by coming to sit with you in the workshop and ask, 'this one, na wetin; that one na wetin; show me wetin you change'. Not the ones who want to follow you to where you bought the spare parts. Those ones are bad market. You must avoid them like a debtor avoids his creditor. When they come tell them you are busy. The women you must prefer are good trusting women who call you to take their car. Those ones call to monitor progress only asking: 'dat one na how much?' And that is all you need to hear, "how much?" That is what puts a smile on your greasy face. That is when you invent parts and problems that do not exist and inflate the prices of the ones that do. This is not wrong; your conscience must not judge you. She is only paying for the ease with which she does business with you. After all do people not go to hotels and buy a bottle of beer for five times the market value? Why don't they complain? God will judge those who sit in their offices and say bad things about you.

The people who come for regular checks or servicing, these ones are not your main target. You do not make much from the engine oil and oil filter. People who are very careful about their cars like that are usually stingy. But you need that steady flow of money, so keep them. However, there is a way to deal with the really stingy ones. Just notice a problem. Tell them that, it is not so serious, but in the near future it will need to be worked on. Even though you have told him that it is OK for now, you have already planted the seeds in his heart. Forget to tie some bolt or tie it loosely. In about a week it will come off and his car will stop on the way. He will call you and describe the problem to you. This is when you will remind him that you had mentioned it before. He will feel guilty and foolish. And when a stingy man feels guilty, he temporarily stops being stingy.

If you finish fixing a car in the evening, never call the owner. Try all you can to make the car stay overnight. Especially on a Saturday. Especially when Sikirat, the daughter of the woman selling agbo who is your new girlfriend, has told you of this gbedu she needs to attend. You need a car for this. The customer will understand when you tell him that you do not like to rush your work. The problems of the car were so much that you had to "drop engine". He may grumble, but Sikirat will get driven to her gbedu and will show her gratitude afterwards. Try not to bash the car or forget Sikirat's things in the back.

Spare parts are where to make a killing. Nnamdi, your favourite spare parts dealer, knows how this works. He knows that you have certain customers who always demand to see receipts. He knows to ask you how much to write, or even give you a blank receipt. Nnamdi and his boy Emeka don't care as long as they get paid. You laugh when the receipt-demanding customers stare hard into the paper to make sure they have not been cheated.

When a customer complains about how expensive the spare parts are, tell them, if they like they can go buy it themselves. Tell them where they can get it — all you want is to fix the car. Say that in fact if he buys the spare parts he will lighten your burden. Most people will be satisfied that you are not trying to cheat and just give you the money. But some are stubborn and will visit the spare parts dealer. Don't panic. Nnamdi and Emeka know how to deal with those ones. They will have so much problems that eventually they will realise that they were kobo wise, Naira foolish. You don't like Nnamdi and Emeka, but they understand the business.

To keep a new customer, especially the ones you think will not be stingy, you must impress them. Fix their problem quickly and tell them that in fact you noticed that three bolts were missing which you replaced. Tell them the implication of those missing bolts. It is God who made them come because it might have caused bigger damage. But you are not charging for the bolts, just being a good mechanic. As they struggle to count the cash, tell them how some mechanics are shoddy like that, forgetting to put back bolts and all. You are not like that. You take your time and solve both seen and unseen problems.

When a customer comes the first time and you want to keep them, never tell them how much your "labour" or "workmanship" is. Tell them, 'Oga, just gimme anything'. He is bound to be grateful for all the extra things which you emphasise you did for free; for saving him from his last evil mechanic. He is bound to be generous. Even if he isn't, you have already made a killing from the spare parts.

As you work, I pray that God will intervene in your greasy hustle and bless it, immensely.

HOW TO BE A NIGERIAN WRITER

You know the value of books. The process of making them intrigues you. You want your name on the front cover of a book and, like an earthworm inches through dirt into the ground, you want to make your way into people's homes, heads and hearts. I am here to help you achieve that.

The African Writer's Look

First, you must look the part. It is important to look like an African writer. Find multi-coloured kampala fabric and use it to sew shirts which you'll wear to all writers' events. Or an old t-shirt. You shouldn't look like a model or banker. Your precious time is spent thinking of plot and theme and words, not on dress and grooming. Your hair needs to be unkempt. However, nothing says authentic-tortured-African-writer like dreadlocks. Please, note that in Nigeria there is a difference between dreadlocks and 'dada'. Dada is less refined, naturally matted coils of hair due to superstitious neglect. Dada is uncool. Dreadlocks are deliberate. They are cool. They make you look wildly creative. If someone asks; no, you are not a Rastafarian. You are an African writer.

Vice and the Writer

As a writer, you must flaunt your vices. You need to show that you are a flawed character. If you drink, drink too much. If you smoke, do it at inappropriate times. Show up at an event reeking of booze. People will understand. People will even understand if you are a male writer who sexually harasses women. Just call your actions a writer's excesses. Vices are a tool of the trade.

Now, you have the basic tools: a multi-coloured kampala shirt, cool dreadlocks, and vices. You must set about the business of writing.

Reading is not synonymous with Writing

You do not need to read a lot to be a Nigerian writer. In fact, as a Nigerian writer you can make shameless statements like "I don't really read much", "I don't want to be tainted by other people's words jamming my own" in public. All you need is a burning desire to write. It is sufficient to have read Shakespeare and Achebe, and maybe a little of Chimamanda Adichie for contemporary reading. The only thing you need to really study is a dictionary or thesaurus. Please, note that all Nigerian characters are Africans who act the same: children are respectful of elders; parents are always responsible, wise individuals teaching children valuable lessons of life. Characters do not use cuss words or talk about sex, even when in the company of peers. Nobody's mother smokes and we have no homosexuals in Nigeria.

Use big words instead of small words; "discombobulate" instead of "confuse". How can you write like a layperson when you are a Nigerian writer? It doesn't matter how many people read or understand you. What matters is that you impress those who do.

Use many words. It is always better to err on the side of verbosity than to err on the side of brevity.

Criticism

Protect your work fiercely and always insist that people give you constructive criticism. Anyone who points out, rightly or otherwise, that your writing isn't quite there yet, is evil and an enemy of your hustle. You must believe that there is nothing like bad writing. After all, you were inspired by the spirits before you began writing — what do critics know?

Editors

Do not waste your time or money on editors. Editors are failed writers whose life ambition is to frustrate the hustle of real writers like you. Show your friends your work. But only the ones who are not jealous of your hustle, and who remind you that your writing is the best thing since point-and-kill. Find some popular person from your village who will write you a foreword without actually reading your book. Then, go to press.

Printing

Go to Ibadan or Lagos. Find a cheap printer who can print 1,000 copies without ink smearing or the pages coming out lopsided. Arrange for a transporter to bring your book home.

The Book Launch

A book is not complete without a book launch. In Nigeria, a book launch is a fund-raising ceremony. It is not important to have writers at this event. Well, maybe the book reviewer. You need your state governor (who may not come but will send a representative with a cheque or a pledge); your Local Government chairman; your Pastor or Imam to bless the event; and any minister, senator or rich person that you know. It is important to find a Chief Launcher who will encourage others to donate to your hustle. Do not leave it to chance or the discretion of the Chief Launcher, unless you are sure of his capabilities. In Nigeria, nobody is allowed to embarrass the Chief Launcher by giving more money. So, if you can, gently hint that you know he will set the bar high for others to follow. That is the job of the Chief Launcher – setting the bar as high as possible.

Marketing and Publicity

You do not need a marketer, publicist or publisher. These people eat into your profit margin. If you have a car, carry a few hundred copies in the trunk at all times. Be your own marketer. Steer conversation toward your book and tell them you have written this really cool book. Someone will ask for it and you will tell them to hold on for a minute while you get it from your car. If you don't have a car, have a big bag that can carry at least ten copies. Do not be ashamed to carry your books to public gatherings. Book by book, God blessing your hustle, you may end up selling off the 1,000 copies your printer produced, and maybe even go for a reprint.

Awards

Get an award. It doesn't matter what. It may be from your church bulletin which you have been writing for since you were in secondary school or your old boys' association newsletter. You can even have friends get together to organise and award you the "Roforofo Prize for African Fiction". Then, you can have on your book, 'Award-Winning Author'. No need to state what award it is. An award-winning writer is a good writer.

It is my hope that you make it as a writer and have many

successful books in the market. And with well-organised book launchings, you can be sure that God will bless your hustle.

HOW TO BE A JOURNALIST

If you ask me, you have the best profession in the world. And especially as a Nigerian journalist, even though your bosses never pay you, you have so much potential to make it in this life. I have taken my time with this one, only because of my dedication to your hustle.

As a Nigerian journalist you must recognise that people appreciate the good work that you do. That is why they provide souvenirs and other freebies at events. You must collect as many of the freebies that come your way. It is these freebies that will eventually make you a "branded journalist".

As a fully branded journalist you wear the face cap you got from covering the Cancer Awareness Walk on International Cancer Day. You use the fancy pen from the speech and prize giving day of a British school in Abuja. Your notepads — all seven of them — are from different seminars; you prefer the one you got from the Section on Business Law Conference. Your flash drive is from an Oil and Gas seminar — you like the Oil and Gas people because they are not stingy with souvenirs or food and drinks. Your bag is from the National Conference of the Nigerian Society of Engineers; you know how conference bags don't last, so you look forward to another conference this year. You have white, blue, yellow and orange t-shirts from the unveiling of new companies, product launches and company anniversaries. Your shiny key holder is from covering the Annual General Meeting of a bank.

You need branding. To help in your branding process, I am hereby making a call on companies and organizations to stop being stingy and step up their souvenirs to include jeans, belts and sneakers (or palm sandals). Wouldn't it be nice to have it all?

Now you must watch out for stingy people. Some obscure group invites you to cover a symposium with a dangerous topic like "Curbing the Boko Haram Menace". You take the risk, dust your Cancer Walk fez cap and iron your orange 10-year anniversary t-shirt. You reach there and find to your shock that the high table has only bottled water. This can't be good. If the high table has bottled water, they will serve pure water to the audience. But you stay and cover the event, do the interviews. When the time comes for you to leave, the organizers greet you with big grateful handshakes and smiles and tell you they look forward to seeing their event on air or in the papers. Someone gives you his card. They ask for yours. You don't have a card but you tear a sheet of paper from the Business Law Conference notepad and write your number. They walk away. Nothing. No food in take away packs. No "thank you" envelopes. No souvenirs! You think of the money you paid the motorcyclist to get here; the way you argued because he didn't think the hall was this far from the junction; the way you shouted and told him if he didn't know his way around Lagos, he had no business being a motorcyclist. Something has to happen to those tapes and interviews. They will buy all the newspapers tomorrow and watch your TV station until their eyes hurt. They will see NOTHING. Just like you saw nothing. Because that is what happens to ingrates.

One of your sacred duties as a Nigerian journalist is to connive with the authorities when it comes to figures of fatalities.

Nigerians are bad with numbers and they have bad tempers. If you give them the real figures of how many Muslims or Christians or Igbos or Hausas were killed they will go and start another round of killing. So, when 500 people are killed in that village, you must report the official figure of 16. It is better.

Make no mistake about it, you need to sell newspapers. Good headlines make good sales. If your paper sells in the North for example and a non-Northern Boko Haram member is caught you must find out and include his tribe in the headline. "Yoruba Boko Haram Kingpin Complete With Tribal Marks Nabbed in Kaura-Namoda". Just like tribe is everything, a headline is everything.

Sometimes you will be fortunate and land a cool job as a senior guy in a media organization. You will get to anchor a discussion program. Important people will be on your program. You must not do any research that will spoil your ability to think on your feet. You need to argue with your guest and interrupt him as much as possible when he is speaking. Butt in with your own views and suggestions. Nigerians like it when two people are speaking at the same time. They will enjoy the interview. After all, why be on TV if you can't say your mind?

If you get really fortunate, and I pray you do, you will be discovered by the almighty foreign media and they will make you a stringer — one of those guys they phone when they hear we have been bombed. Then you will be able to sell our bad news in exchange for the title 'International Journalist'. Some people may dislike you and call you a snitch that shows our dirty linen to foreign media. God will judge them. Bad news sells; it is not your fault that you get paid in crisp Western Union dollars to send in pictures and stories of bombings. Pray to be within driving distance when there is a bomb or shooting. That way you can quickly get there and do a phone interview and get paid. The more bad news, the more dollars. Foreigners don't need to hear our boring good news. It is a job, and unfortunately, like the undertaker, bad things must happen for you to make money. God sees your good heart.

And if in the end, to crown your success, a government sees fit to reward your loyalty by making you their official spokesperson or a Special Assistant on Media, to God be the glory. You must take this job seriously. Attack free speech and any other journalists who may want to print truth about your principal. Be creative with facts. Denounce unfavourable reports as fake news and warn people not to insult your principal on social media. Your principal will be impressed. When finally your government's tenure is over, you will have earned enough to take a break, pay for a short course at Harvard or some other American university and write a tell-all book about your time in power which will tell everything except how you were implicated in any scandals. Then return to Nigeria and launch that book to the glory of God and for the benefit of mankind. God bless your hustle!

HOW TO BE A KIDNAPPER

I hope this finds you well. If so, doxology. I am not trying to teach you your job. If you are already calling yourself a kidnapper or contemplating it, it means that you already have things figured out. The very reason you have become so popular in today's Nigeria is that all is not well. I get that. When I say I hope this finds you well, I mean that in spite of all the problems — some of which have driven you to this profession (forgive me if you have a day job which you prefer to call your profession) — I hope you are somehow ok, health wise and all. Because being ill and doing the hard work of kidnapping can pose a serious challenge. You don't want to have a bladder infection while managing an abduction. In short, I am wishing that you are in good health or at least a state of health that will not jeopardise your business. This chapter is to make sure that you understand me and my needs as your potential client.

You see, unlike many Nigerians, my head is not buried in the sand. I will not be shocked when you kidnap me. I will not express anger. I will not even break down in tears. I will not pee in my pants (except if you kidnap me just after drinking and refuse to let me use the bathroom). I will not have any of the reactions which I assume you have become accustomed to. (I hope that you have some experience in this kidnapping business because I would hate to deal with a beginner: beginners panic and do things like shoot the people they have abducted. If you are new, I will advise you to calm down. I am not going to be a problem. We can work through this together. Like they say, with God all things are possible.)

The reason I will be calm is quite simple. I am a Nigerian that has common sense. I also read. I know how hard things are becoming. I also know how ungoverned Nigeria is. So whether it has become easier to kidnap people or life has become harder or both, I understand. Also, we both know the police is not going to get involved under any circumstances except perhaps to make sure the ransom money is secure so yeah, I am not going to call them. None of my people are going to contact the police either. If we are going to have to spend money, better to give it to you, than pay for "fuel" and paper to write the statement then still end up paying the ransom. My point is, calm down and let us negotiate.

I want you to be reasonable. I am not suggesting you are unreasonable. God forbid. I was raised in a good Christian home and I cannot accuse a brother falsely. You are my brother, let us not argue, even if you are from Cameroon. We are all brothers. Unless you are white – not that I am racist but I know you are not white. I am only saying that I am encouraging you to do what you normally would have done, which is, be reasonable.

I want you to understand that even though you may have read my name or the name of my book in the New York Times or The Guardian UK, it does not mean anything. I have no money. Despite what anyone tells you, writers are poor. My publishers give me only 10% of the profit per book. And let's be honest, I can never know how many books my publisher actually sells. If they tell me they sold only 100, I can't prove they sold thousands. This 10% book business is not much better than hawking Gala and La Casera and pure water and scotch egg in traffic. (I don't understand people who eat scotch egg in public transport in traffic. They stink up the bus and they look silly opening their mouths wide to bite into it. If not that you can't get much out of them, I would have said those are the kind of people who deserve to be kidnapped. Those ones and the agents of darkness who eat moin-moin in offices and on buses.) Plus, when the advance on my book came in 2016, I took more than half of it and paid it to my landlord in Abuja. If you had not already gone through the trouble of kidnapping me, I would have suggested that you should have taken my Abuja landlord instead of me. Or one of those annoying neighbours with a loud generator. Or you take my publisher, who in the end makes far more money than I do.

My point is, I am a poor writer. All those countries you see me going to, I don't pay for it. There are nice people in many countries who have read my book and pay for me to come and read there. They don't even really pay. They just buy my ticket and give a couple hundred dollars as a per diem (if I am lucky) and by the time you have gone out twice abroad, the money is all finished. You can't even buy a decent perfume at the airport on your way back. And you know how Nigerians are. Once they know you travelled abroad, there will be a queue outside your house of people waiting for gifts. Some will even send you a list (without money). And if you ignore them, they will say you are proud. They will remind you of the time nobody knew you and only them cared about you. They will call you ungrateful.

I also do not have a rich family. My father is a retired civil servant and my mother, well, unless you can sell her clothes and hair products, there is no money to be made there. (I had heard that my mother had other richer suitors, but why my mother chose to marry a poor man is a story for another day). So, just ask for a little money and we can all be happy.

However, while the negotiations are going on, I have a few requests. Notice I didn't say demands. Your ransom is a demand which, don't get me wrong, you deserve. I am only begging. As a writer, I want to at least make something out of the kidnapping experience. I need to write about it. You make the ransom money, I make some good writing and fame out it. At-all at-all na im bad pass. If possible, I want a selfie. Because you know how our generation is. If there is no photo or video or link, it did not happen. You can die these days and the children of the devil on the internet will ask your family announcing it for photos or links so they can believe you are truly dead. I already said I won't do anything funny like try to call the police. We both know how useless that is (this is not an American film where their police trace kidnapper calls and show up commando style). And really, I expect that as a professional you would have blindfolded me on the way to your business premises. Or we can just use an actual digital camera. If you don't have one we can buy one — just take the money from the ransom when you get it. Or ask, as a preliminary demand before actual negotiations that they send a camera. (If it wasn't too much to ask, I might have asked if you would let me sneak a couple of my own demands into your list of demands. But you alone worked for this kidnapping and I won't just come and ride on your hustle. That would be opportunistic. You know, like when a woman struggled with some rough guy for over a decade, patiently cleaned him up, married and made him decent, and then some random woman sees him on the street corner and thinks he was always this wonderful and tries to snatch him. Or like all those criminals who got elected across the country by affixing Buhari's photo to their campaign posters. That kind of opportunistic. God forbid.)

One good suggestion is to play some games while we are waiting. I find that boredom kills. Look at the damage our bored legislators do because there is no real work to be done; making music videos, having threesomes, padding budgets and all. I suggest Ludo. Or WHOT. Also, talk to me. I want to hear your story. I will tell you mine. That you kidnapped me does not mean we can't gist a little. You may find that we have more in common than you ever imagined.

(And please don't worry about food. I am not proud. I have no special dietary requirements. I will eat what you eat. And since everyone is worried about equality and diversity these days, have you thought of having female members in your kidnapping company – or more female members if you already have some? That would be great.)

God bless your hustle. And may you or your loved ones never, ever be kidnapped.

LAW AND LAW ENFORCEMENT

HOW TO BE A LAWYER

Life is challenging. There is a reason your poor family decided to pool resources to send you to Law School. They didn't send you there to take the long route — serving some stingy senior lawyer or law firm for 5-10 years before you can afford to make it on your own. (I will treat the issue of stingy senior lawyers another day.)

When people ask me how it feels like to be a lawyer, I often save them from the disappointment that the truth is sure to give them; I shrug, smile and add to whatever mystery already exists in their head.

But you my faithful reader — especially you the new lawyer or law student — I will tell the truth. I want you to at least, like your banker colleagues, be able to afford to pay your own rent and buy a clean second-hand car in the first to second year of your call to the Nigerian Bar.

Register your private law firm as soon as you finish and print your letter head and complimentary cards. Your cards especially should have your full and imposing title: Barrister and Solicitor of the Supreme Court of Nigeria. I mean a lawyer knows that's all hot air but to a non-lawyer it makes you seem like you learnt under Saint Paul himself and have your office right in the Supreme Court. Hustling must start immediately whether you work in a law firm or not.

Learn how to eavesdrop on people's conversation for any possible legal services they may need. Somebody's wife was slapped. Apologise for butting in, then quickly inform them that under our legal system, that is a crime called assault. You are a lawyer and you can help them. By help you mean take their money. If they look at you funny, whip out your card. They will see that full title which is a killer. Suddenly you will appear more intelligent, more important.

When you walk into a big store, don't just buy stuff and leave. If you can see the manager, ask if they have registered their business with the Corporate Affairs Commission. Company registration is a no-brainer. Yes, serious lawyers snub it and all but what do you care? Offer to register their business for less than what your colleagues charge. The whole idea is turnover. If you have many companies to register at the same time, it won't matter that you are charging less (and spoiling business for other hustling lawyers).

You must never ignore police stations. There is always money to be made there. Anyone who calls you a charge and bail lawyer, God will consume them by fire. Take keen interest in the affairs of your neighbours. There is always someone dragging someone to the police station or someone being arrested for something. Don't wait until you are called. Go there and offer your services. Trouble is your business.

The art of securing bail is one that only the streetwise can handle. No one will teach you that in school. They teach you crap like "bail is free" and "no one must be held for more than 24 hours without charge". Bah! The police in Nigeria don't care what you've been taught, in fact, the more legal you get, the more complicated things get for your prospective client. And trust me there is nothing worse than messing up a neighbour's case. You don't want to be sneaking into your own neighbourhood at odd hours. I have only, in my few years of legal practice, secured one free bail. And that was only because the DPO was on the Investigating Police Officer's (IPO) case for something else. I cashed in on his confusion and by the time he realised I was not going to give him any money, my client had been released and bond papers signed. He however took me to the side and gave me a good talking to: 'na you make your client no give us anything abi? Ok! Ok! Ok!'

Moral of the story? 1. Common sense is more useful than law inside a police station. 2. You have no friends inside a police station. 3. Bail is hardly ever free.

You must learn how to negotiate with the Investigating Police Officer (IPO), firmly, respectfully and pragmatically. Learn this and you will become a hot cake in your community, making so much money that you won't care if anyone calls you charge and bail.

To avoid the stereotypical look of the struggling Nigerian lawyer — shirts that were once white, shoe soles eaten to a 45-degree angle, a heavy tattered bag containing everything from your wig and gown to dozens of company registration forms and affidavit forms — you need to also be an estate agent. You must befriend as many landlords as you can so that you will have signboards reading 'TO LET' on as many empty houses as possible.

Look for people trying to sell houses or land and help them aggressively market it. You never know which 10% commission will take you permanently out of poverty. When you have sold that expensive house and ride home in a Range Rover Sport (with NBA stickers in front and behind) no one will bother if you ever go to court or not. Your neighbours will hail you as you drive past: 'Barristaa!'

It is no surprise that struggling lawyers are the most hated in their families. The reason is simple. After supporting you morally and otherwise to become a lawyer, the least they expect from you is to make reasonable contributions at family events and send money into their accounts when they call you.

God forbid that you become a struggling Nigerian lawyer. Follow my advice and your family and neighbours will think you are the best thing since Saturday banking. As always, God bless your hustle.

HOW TO BE A POLICE OFFICER

You didn't know it would be like this when you were applying. You just knew you wanted a job. Your relatives came together and contributed the money you put in an envelope to grease the wheels that would roll you through the various recruitment levels. Money that was probably going to be bigger than your first salary. But no amount of money is too big for the privilege of wearing that uniform.

You were excited about the new uniform. About the rank. The serial number. Your name on your breast. But no one told you. No one whispered it into your ear that you would be serving an ungrateful, hateful bunch of people who think you are the worst thing since discovering palm oil on your white shirt as you walk into school on a Monday morning.

You do not understand the hate. You cannot make sense of the lies they tell about you. But you will do your duty and serve your fatherland (or is it motherland you can never tell) in spite of all the naysayers and bad belle people. You will be a police officer.

The Checkpoint

God forbid that they put you on checkpoint duty. Someone has to do it. Someone has to flag down cars and shine a weak torch into people's faces. Someone has to salute the people in nice cars and remind them that their "boys are loyal". And especially on the weekend, someone has to wish the law-abiding citizens "happy weekend". Who else will give road users the privilege of showing their appreciation for the selfless work you do, with a bit of cash? You are not doing anything wrong. Think if there were no beggars in Nigeria. If they all went on strike. All those people who go to marabouts and juju priests would have nowhere to give up the offerings that form part of the rituals. You perform a serious duty. Take it seriously. Raise your voice when you ask: "Anything for the boys?" or "Oga how e go be na?" or "Madam de Madam!" Be proud of who you are. Be confident. Look people in the eye. Don't squeeze the notes you receive. Fold them nicely, put it in your front pocket and slap it gently to make it sit comfortably. God sees your heart.

The Station

People may scrunch up their noses when they walk into a police station without asking, "Why does this place smell like an abandoned public secondary school male toilet on a Friday afternoon?" They will not ask why the walls have to look like a kitchen of a motor park bukka. They will judge you over a small thing like filth and stench. Your intention is not to make anyone comfortable in there. You want the suspects to reflect. To think of the crime they may or may not have done. To be so moved by all of the sights and smells to repentance. To come to a point where they hate crime. The people who judge you do not understand that as a police officer you are a literary person. The walls and floors are a metaphor for the hearts of the criminals: dirty. You want to hold up a mirror to them. You do it for their own good. You do not want a nice comfortable police station where people will commit crimes just to spend the night as if it were a motel. God forbid that your station becomes a motel. (It does not matter if they are innocent. The fact that they got arrested means that at least, they followed bad gangs. And did someone important not say: show me your friends and I will tell you the kind of person you are?)

And you know, if you ask me, I would introduce a standard fee for paper when people need to write a statement. You do not fetch paper from the street. People should stop being stingy and support your station with the right kind of stationery.

The Pot Belly

You may start out thin and flat bellied. Do not see that as a thing of pride. You will look awkward with your police uniform tucked into a thin waist with your stomach looking like a chalk board. People won't respect you if you look hungry. Whether you are male or female, this applies to you. You need to slowly work your way to making your uniform look good and make the journey around your large belly. That way you look like authority and when you tuck in your uniform, you look menacing enough to stop crime. God forbid a flat, hungry belly. It will not be your portion.

The Patrol Vehicle

Like I said, you are a literary person. You are deep. Your patrol vehicle is another example of a symbol and a metaphor all in one. Don't mind the people who watch Hollywood movies and want to bring fiction into reality, wanting police patrol vehicles to look nice and neat, complete with bumpers and fenders, rear lights, windshields and a radio that works. Your patrol vehicle is a metaphor for the struggle of society.

The dents are a metaphor for the deep impressions you want to make on people. The broken indicator is a metaphor for all the broken things which indicate how problematic crime can be, broken things which you intend to fix. Your job is to fight crime, not have a nice car. Leave nice cars for politicians. Nobody has time for that. Do not bother with replacing lights. Hold together broken or cracked bumpers with nice thick copper wire. You are like that copper wire, holding the fabric of society together. And for this God will bless you.

The Barracks

As a humble person, you do not care about looking flashy. The barracks is where people can best see your humility. In the open sewers. In the litter. In the bushes and shrubs. In the half-naked children everywhere. The barracks have to show how down to earth you are. So down to earth you do not care about kempt surroundings. If you see someone obsessively cutting grass, cleaning the gutters, bearing children responsibly or sweeping the streets, it is a sign that they don't have work to do. And we all know that the idle mind is the devil's workshop. May God never let you become a workshop for the devil.

The Discipline

People don't understand you. To get well-shaped metal tools the blacksmith must beat it into shape. The blacksmith doesn't beat the red-hot iron because he hates it. Far from it. The blacksmith beats it out of love for the craft of making metal tools and items. Same with gold. It has to go through fire for purity. When you slap a suspect or chain them or beat them until you get a confession or slam batons onto the soles of their feet or strip them naked or whip them or let other cell mates beat them or electrocute them through their penis (if PHCN allows), you do it out of love. Same way a mother will let a nurse insert a needle into the buttocks of her child. An injection hurts. But a mother knows it will help the child in the long run. You, more than most people know this. And it is not like you even go that far. You will never insert anything into another person's buttocks. You love the people you torture... I mean, discipline. You want them to change. You want them to confess and write that statement that will make the case end quickly. God, who sees your heart, knows this and will reward you greatly.

The Accidental Discharge

No, I don't mean when you accidentally ejaculate into a sex worker you have arrested behind a police van. Sometimes as a police officer, you will shoot people accidentally. Like when you have drunk too much alomo bitters during the night patrol. You need the alomo. The night is cold and full of errors. And guns are unpredictable. Don't let this affect the love you have for your job. Don't let a small thing like an accidental discharge or killing someone at a checkpoint stop you from giving your life to changing society.

Bail

See ba, people are ungrateful. If someone helps them carry load in the motor park or in the market, do they just walk away? Don't they give them something? In fact, these days the motor park touts negotiate their fee very aggressively before they even touch your load. No one sees anything wrong with that. In the old days people helped people. If they can pay a tout why should they not pay a law enforcement officer? Are they saying that a tout deserves more than a person who risks their life to protect society? Yes, bail is free but you are only asking people to be reasonable. Just some appreciation, the way they would appreciate any other hard-working person they meet. May God send sensible lawyers who have home training and know how to show appreciation when you finally release their clients. I mean they could have been accidentally shot. Or died in a shootout with you. You know how those criminals like shootouts, sometimes even with handcuffs or ropes binding their hands they will dare to engage you in one. God forbid that you are forced into a shootout.

I have heard rumours like police officers working with armed robbers and sharing the proceeds, renting out guns, asking for money to help recover stolen property, raping sex workers without condoms after arresting them, helping politicians harass people who disrespect them, disappearing people. Rumours are the work of the devil and his children. (People should stop allowing the devil to use them). I do not take them very seriously. You shouldn't either because no one can prove that any of it is true.

God bless your hustle as you serve and protect everyone, including ungrateful, rumour-peddling Nigerians.

POLITRICKING

HOW TO BE A POLITICIAN

The biggest mistake any person interested in politics can make is to apply rules generally applicable to regular human beings to Nigeria. Often, Nigerians in the diaspora wishing to return home to enter politics assume that just because they are black or have a green passport, they can fit right in. This is a manual for persons hoping to avoid embarrassment as they enter politics in Nigeria.

God

This is the first and most important thing. A Nigerian politician must understand how to tap into and use God, both in times of peace and times of trouble. This is because with God, all things are possible — from the relocation of funds from public coffers into your private accounts to making sure that you get more votes from a polling unit than the number of human beings who are registered to vote. The latter is not strange. Do not let anyone make you feel bad about it. Did Jesus not take five loaves of bread and two fish and multiply it until it could feed five thousand people in Bethsaida?

A good Nigerian politician knows how to use God for protection. So, for example when you want the people not to revolt against you, remind people that you were sent by God. Declare that you could never have entered office without God leading you by the hand and personally giving you the seat.

Those who voted — including those who adjusted figures and thumb-printed on ballots — are nothing but biros in the hand of God. They should know that no one gets power unless by God's permission. This will make anyone afraid of questioning the authority of God.

God is also important when you have just won an election and you need to blackmail the out-rigged opponent. Give an acceptance speech saying that you thank God for giving you the victory; say that you cannot question God who decided that you were the only person fit for that office. Your opponent will feel bad and let it go. God is great.

However, you need to know when not to use God. If you have a task that you doubt you will be able to perform, say, 'I will do everything humanly possible', to remind them that although God is personally involved in giving you power, they should not be disappointed if you fail. Because you are only human.

Branding

Your hustle as a politician involves a lot of branding. Forget the elitist social media people who make fun of politicians who brand bags of rice. Those people do not vote. They sit in Abuja, Lagos and Port Harcourt with their iPads and expensive smartphones, making noise. Some of them do not even live in Nigeria. The real Nigerians who vote, not only do not mind, they expect it. They expect to receive items like mint sweets, coffee mugs, t-shirts, small bags of rice, beans, flour, sugar or salt, exercise books, pens, phones, bottled water (or sachet water depending on how poor your constituents are) and rechargeable lanterns branded with your name and/or photo.

The Godfather

Unless you ARE the godfather, you always NEED to have a godfather. If you do not realise this then you are standing on slippery ground. The identification of an appropriate godfather is the beginning of political wisdom. Show your loyalty by donating money at events organised by your godfather or his children and close relatives. If your godfather's child is getting married, you must make sure your large donation is seen and acknowledged. If your godfather is running for office you must sponsor billboards with his large photo and your small one in the corner where it says "Courtesy: Someone-whose-loyalty-needs-to-be-noticed."

If you ever meet your godfather's wife or child at a shop, whether in Nigeria or abroad, make sure you pay for whatever they buy. Even if they say no, insist. Beg if you must. Tell them if they do not let you pay, you will kill yourself.

Pay for full page colour ads in newspapers on their birthdays and call them a blessing to all of humankind.

A godfather can be the blessing to your hustle or the tool of your downfall. Never ever allow anyone to print your photo in the same size as that of your godfather on the same billboard or newspaper ad. Your photo must always be smaller and beneath that of the godfather.

Social Media

Now I know I have said those people on social media are good-for-nothing. I insist that in real voting terms, they are useless. But it is important to have people who fight for you in the media. In Nigeria there is no good or evil. There is only for and against. An evil person is one that has no one fighting for them. There is poverty and unemployment in the land, so getting people to post tweets and Facebook posts for you is not very expensive. Many will even do it for free. Avoid those hustlers who call themselves social media consultants. They just know how to blow grammar. All you need are motivated guys who have internet connection and the hope that when their oga's hustle is blessed, it will reach them. It is these ones who will identify any bad thing said about you and attack appropriately.

Scandals

When a real scandal happens, like say, foreign police catch you with stolen money, or people identify you as a sponsor of terrorism, the best thing to do is nothing. It does not matter how bad it is. Those who support you do not need your explanation, and those who demand an explanation will never support you. Plus, Nigerians have the shortest memories among human beings worldwide. Just be patient, and they will forget everything. It is more important to forget than to forgive. Of what good is forgiveness if people can remember the wrong that was done? That is why Nigeria is such a great place for politics. Yesterday's murderer can become tomorrow's statesman.

Catch Phrases

There are phrases that every Nigerian politician must use. I will give you a list which is by no means exhaustive:

Dastardly act

Campaign of calumny

Nascent democracy

Gratitude to God Almighty

All hands are on deck

I have set up a committee

I remain committed

God (As in God-sent, God-willing, God's grace etc.)

Shame

Do you sometimes feel shame when you are caught doing something wrong? If the answer is yes, then you are not ready for Nigerian politics. Can you look at a crowd when you are caught with your fingers in a pot of soup, and tell them, while licking your fingers, that in fact, you have never entered a kitchen in your life, talk less of a pot of soup? No? Then you are not ready for Nigerian politics. A good Nigerian politician who is caught on camera stuffing wads of dollar notes into his cap, knows how to say 'it wasn't me' without blinking. Nigerian supporters, especially those of your tribe or religion, do not need evidence of your innocence. Once they support you, they themselves will come up with reasons why you cannot be guilty.

Religion

Do you have doubts about the existence of God? Keep it to yourself. If you have a Christian background, find a few churches and start attending. Go to Jerusalem. Take a photo there and hang it in your office. If you have a Muslim background, then make sure you are visible at least once a week at Friday prayers. Go for the Hajj. It does not matter that when you are on holiday in London or America you enjoy bacon and lots of alcohol. Appearance is everything. Nigerians would rather a fornicating, lying, thieving Christian or Muslim, than a clean atheist. Keep your other beliefs to yourself but claim one of the two foreign religions.

It is important to always have a good friend of the other acceptable religion. That friend will come in handy when people accuse you of favouring only people of your own religion or of being a fanatic. If you can't find a friend, then have employees of the other religion, like a cook or driver. Otherwise, sleep with women of the other religion. That way, if someone says you are a fanatic, just say, if I hated the other religion, would I have slept with their women?

Caps/Hats

You may take this for granted, but close your eyes for a minute and think of a successful Nigerian politician who doesn't wear a cap? When was the last time you saw the bare head of a Nigerian president? I don't know what it is about a cap, but it cannot be a coincidence that everyone, from our founding fathers to the current destructive fathers, wears a cap/hat. Better to be safe than sorry. Find a cap or hat and wear it often.

Fitness

Especially if you plan to be a legislator at the state and federal level, it is important to be fit and strong for the occasional fights that will break out. You don't want to be the one who ends up in hospital after a fight in a House of Assembly. Everyone has a phone with a camera these days and it would be a tragedy if you were caught on camera unable to fight back. Sometimes also our democracy means that you may need to break maces or climb over parliamentary gates. If you are currently unfit, register in a gym or start doing yoga.

Follow these tips and I assure you, you will be properly positioned for God to bless your political hustle.

HOW TO BE FIRST LADY

People underestimate the power in the cliché, "Behind every successful man, there is a woman". You know the useful variations of that cliché, like "behind every successful man is a sensible woman". Sensible because there are women behind and in front who are never seen. We all know how men are. They can't make up their minds as to what they want, whether it is the wife, the wife's friend, the girlfriends, or the housemaid. It is your job to make sure he keeps you in your proper place: by his side, as First Lady.

You do not confront him about the other women you and half the world know he has. In fact, officially, your husband is a kind, God-fearing man incapable of carnal knowledge against the order of marriage (or of nature). You say this as often as you can.

You showed early interest in politics. This is what separated you from the other women — the ability to support his career. You didn't need plenty of degrees for this. You didn't even need to know how to speak English well. Wisdom saved you — you got into the field, attended party rallies and didn't show signs of sleep deprivation or irritation. It was clear to you that during election campaigns, primaries and elections proper, you would be expected to show stamina, stay up all night campaigning, counting votes, manufacturing votes, or waiting for results. You did. You won.

Now that you have crossed the preliminary hurdles, it is time to think of your public image. This is where I come in. Listen.

The pet project is a blessing in disguise. People underestimate it, ignore it, misunderstand it, even mock it. It is not their fault. Leave them. They don't understand the potential. Nobody asks questions or checks your budgets. Nobody asks how much you make or spend. It is just like your husband's security vote. Do something for the less privileged, orphans, widows... that kind of thing. Show you are not afraid of poor or disabled children. Let the cameras capture you smiling while you touch a cripple, hug a poor person, pick up an orphan or push someone's wheelchair. This will prove that you really love and care for them. Have NTA show you dancing with them on Children's Day. But don't sweat it. You also need time for other aspects of national politics. The days when first ladies were all about pet projects are over.

Remember that no matter who the Party appoints as women leader, you ARE the de facto women leader, the mummy of the federation. Act like it. Host parties and gala nights for wives of governors, ministers and Party men. Sit at the head of the table.

Be innovative. Take the initiative to touch base with your husband's supporters. Go and thank them for voting him in. It doesn't matter if you cause massive hold-ups while you are at it. That way they know you are in town.

Consolidate your position by supporting one or two people to get appointments in Oga's government. You need an eye there. Flex your muscles once in a while by making someone who has annoyed you in the presidency lose his job. People need to know you are not just a pet project first lady.

However, be careful when you are collecting kickbacks from contractors and those who badly need to see the President for favours. You don't want your husband to leave his serious job of being President to clean up your scandals. Use reliable people to do your money laundering, not people who will blurt out your name the moment they are caught with huge sums of foreign currency.

You are getting older. Take care of yourself. Do complete makeovers if you have to (I hear Dubai is great for makeovers). But be careful. With the exception of harmless Botox injections, avoid needles. Avoid knives and tubes and suction pipes. You don't want to leave your exalted position for some small girl to inherit.

There are people in the media, half-baked journalists and idle bloggers, who will look at everything you do, your head tie, your children, your grammar, your toenails, the texture of your voice. Unfortunately, this is a democracy and you must endure them. But rest assured that God will judge evil journalists, bloggers and Twitter people.

To boost your international image, you need to be seen in glossy magazines with wives of leaders of good countries. Aim high; the American First Lady. My prayer for you is that the Americans don't elect a woman or gay man as president when it is time for your photo.

Finally, don't get carried away. Those men who kneel at your feet today do it only because your husband is alive and in power. If that changes, they will disappear faster than the money in our treasury. People will no longer print wrappers with your photo or use your name to sing local songs. Nobody will even call you to events as ex-First Lady. That future might appear grim, but that is why you must face the serious business of enjoying the present. God bless your hustle, ma.

HOW TO BE AN OPPOSITION POLITICIAN

Our politicians in the ruling party have failed us. And God will address their matter. But before that divine judgment must come the judgment of the people. It is your responsibility as an opposition politician to deliver this well-deserved judgment on behalf of the good and oppressed people of this country.

Your status as opposition politician is attained upon the loss of an election or political post whether or not that post was secured through the ruling party. It is evil for anyone to point to your past and say that you once enjoyed the largesse of the ruling party. What matters is that God has, through your political loss, shown you the light and led you to the honourable path of opposition. Loss of, or failure to secure political office does not an opposition politician make. What completes you as an opposition politician who has lost out in politics is the righteous anger against all the unholy things going on in the government you tried (and failed) to be a part of. There are some who lose out and take the shameful path of hanging around the corridors of power, placing full-page, full-colour pro-government ads in the papers, congratulating every politician in power, commiserating with every serving politician whose grandmother has died. Some even go as far as digging up some dead relative of someone in power to do a 10th year remembrance ad. God forbid that you disgrace yourself like this for political power.

First thing to do is to change political party. You cannot remain in the ruling party and be successful as an opposition politician. Our ruling party does not take kindly to dissidents. They destroy all who try. Look at that small man in the House of Representatives who was trying to be an opposition leader and how they used bribe money to smear and truncate his hustle. So, you must decamp. It may be in a colourful well-attended ceremony where the opposition leaders will welcome you and your supporters in front of cameras or through a press release. It doesn't matter. What matters is that people know you now have nothing to do with the evil big party.

As an opposition politician, you need a platform. You must remain in the consciousness of the people especially now that losing elections has led you to the glorious and honourable path of opposition. Try Twitter. People don't realise how powerful it is. You can, from the comfort of your room, rouse thousands of followers to the holy task of insulting the government. Otherwise, with some "brown envelopes" you can have journalists who will always run your story and give you interviews. If you use Twitter you need a lot of followers. Followers are the key to your success. It is they who will make sure your thoughts get retweeted to the ends of the earth.

Your job as an opposition politician is not difficult. Our country is run like a circus — a lot of what goes on beggars belief. Where else for example will two different security agencies arrest two different sets of suspects who all "confess" to the same crime. Or a government official who will brazenly budget 1.2million for a Facebook account? All you need to do is buy newspapers and follow news reports on Facebook and Twitter. If it is not the President asking us to pray about problems that he needs to solve himself, it is him allocating one billion to the Villa for food. Just tweet it and your thousands of followers will retweet it, adding the necessary insult to injury.

Attack those who disagree with you. Because the opposition should be, like the customer, always right. Those who question your motives or ideas are enemies of progress and agents of the ruling party. They must be denounced. There can be no opposition to the opposition.

You must understand that the only way you can achieve change as an opposition politician is by running for office or getting a political appointment. There is no need to do anything selfless like that Al Gore, who instead of running again for office after he lost, devoted his life to fighting climate change and other environmental causes. That can only work in America. Here you must be in politics to achieve change.

Remember that being an opposition politician covers a multitude of sins, both past and present. As soon as people receive evidence of your having decamped they should, if they are not evil people, turn your crimson past into an immaculate white present. They should not distract you from your task of opposing the government by bringing up scandals and allegations. If they do, the wrath of God shall visit them specially.

I wish you well as an opposition politician and that, someday, God blessing your hustle, you will get that office you so thoroughly deserve.

INTERNATIONAL
CONNECTIONS

HOW TO GET FOREIGN FRIENDS

You love all things foreign. But despite the repeated olive-oiled anointing your pastor gave you and your passport, you failed to get a visa. You failed three times to get visas to America, Canada and Britain. You lost a lot of money trying. After the long, gruelling process, nothing. Not even when you genuinely secured admission to some small college in London. Or took loans to make your bank account look like a solid how-the-hell-can-I-disappear-in-your-country account. God will judge those people who saunter into your country when they please but make you scream your life history at humiliating interviews through a glass that looks like those in prisons in American movies. If only they would have the decency to give you a visa.

You thought of South Africa but after hearing about the deportation of Nigerians and of the xenophobia directed at black Africans, you say to yourself, 'God forbid that I let a fellow black man humiliate me like that. Especially not ones who until the 80's were still being supported by Nigerians in their anti-apartheid struggle.'

God knows you have tried.

You can still mix with Americans. Imagination is a powerful thing. You can have a taste of Canada and all those creamy countries whose visas you have coveted. All here in Nigeria. Granted, the foreigners who come here may not always be the cream of the lot, but beggars cannot be choosers. You will manage the ones here in Abuja. You will enjoy their company so thoroughly that your visa rejections will cease to hurt. After all, is it not people that make a place? My job is to help you learn how to mix with and enjoy the company of foreigners from creamy countries, right here in Nigeria.

You need packaging. Don't look like something they will be scared of. Wear nice clothes and nice French perfume. Something they can relate to. Have a business card that says you do something important or interesting. Nothing introduces you like a nice glossy business card. Work on reducing that heavy accent.

You need to know where to meet foreigners. I can tell you about Abuja at least. Go to play readings and art exhibitions organised by embassies. It doesn't matter if you do not really care about plays or if you think Australian art is just a waste of space. Join the hash. The hash is plenty of white people running or walking, wearing similar colours, drinking plenty beer and doing things you will find very strange. Don't be a bush person. Google the hash and learn their terms. Find out what "Hares", "On-on", or "Down-down" mean. Sometimes there is a small fee you pay. Don't be stingy. Pay up and mix with foreigners.

Watch foreign channels and foreign news to get great conversation starters. Say you meet someone from Belgium, begin by asking her if she is from the Flemish, French or German part. That tells her immediately that you know her country. Then add some random bit of news you recently Googled like, 'So what's this I hear about Brussels planning to fine offensive language?' She will be pleasantly shocked and proceed to give you a lecture about her country, which will soften the ground for future engagements.

When speaking to a foreigner, don't scare them away with

your bush views.

To maintain foreign friends, you need to have foreign thoughts and habits. When you meet British people for example tell them how much you love tea. Say it as if you have always loved tea, as if what you sucked from your mother's breast was steamy tea. You will be shocked at how quickly you will bond. It doesn't matter that it only recently came to you as a rude shock that neither Milo nor Bournvita is tea.

Do not do stupid things like admit that you really do not like homosexuals. You will be blacklisted and all hopes of getting a visa, or foreign friends, will be lost forever.

Never ask for favours. That scares them away. Don't ask for a job or a loan or a lift. As much as they may appear to be in this country to help poor black Nigerians, they do not want needy black friends. Buy your own drinks.

Say you are a poet. Apart from being sexy, a poet is always considered a higher human species. It does not matter that until you read this article you might have asked if Wordsworth was the name of a store. Don't disgrace me. Read. You will see how their eyes will light up once they realise you appreciate the sophisticated things of life.

When you attend a social function organised by white people, do not show up like you do to your Uncle's house, empty handed. Go with something. A bottle of wine. A box of chocolates. That is proper behaviour.

Never, in a moment of frustration, talk about leaving the country. This is disastrous to any friendships you may want to cultivate. Especially if your target works in an Embassy. They will avoid you like flies avoid kerosene. Pretend like if heaven was outside Nigeria, you couldn't care less. They will feel safe.

Make statements that show you have respect for animals. If

he talks about his pet or frets about not finding food for the cat, Archibald, that he brought from Connecticut, be attentive and sympathetic. Remember the cat's name. The next time you meet ask, with a big smile on your face and a hand on his shoulder: 'How is Archibald?'

While you are doing all this, be sure to avoid fellow Nigerians, like cockroaches avoid light. They understand your hustle and will do their best to truncate it. You cannot afford that. You cannot afford some nosy Bulus telling your oyinbo friend, Mr. Carter, whose dog Quentin you religiously ask after, that during Christmas in your village in Kaduna South, you routinely welcome visitors with peppered dog meat.

There is so much I can tell you but follow my advice here. Before long, you will have so many foreign friends that memories of visa humiliations will vanish from your consciousness. And who knows, you might even stumble upon someone from the visa section of a cool country whom God will use to finally bless your hustle.

HOW TO BE A GOOD AFRICAN

Now, I know this is a book about Nigeria. But if you throw a stone into a group of black people you are bound to strike a Nigerian. So, when anyone speaks about Africans, Nigerians being from the most populous country, should be in the front row, taking notes.

I like to think I am a good African — or at least having visited nearly a dozen countries in Africa and Europe, I can say something about what it means to be a good African.

I see it in your eyes, the question: How do I travel to so many countries so quickly? You are right to ask. It is not by paying anyone money. I have no travel agent who secures visas for me. I have no special connections.

I just decided one day to stop being an ordinary African and become a good African. An ordinary African is confined to his/her country or sub-region like a chick in an egg that never hatches. An ordinary African — or, God forbid, a bad African — will never see another country outside their sub-region, except perhaps illegally, by boat or through some desert. In both cases you are as likely to survive as you are likely to receive an email about money from a real Nigerian prince.

We both know you do not desire death. So, swallow your pride and listen.

A good African knows his place

Now, don't take this the wrong way. Knowing your place is simple to understand. You know that the only place where you belong — that is, assuming you are not an undesirable minority or vulnerable person in your own country — is your own country. If you are a skilled professional, especially, you do not want to be a traitor by desiring anything other than living in the country of your birth and origin. Have a conscience. Don't add to the brain drain.

Respect the good men and women who worked on the Khartoum Process and stay in Africa. The Europeans, and especially Germans, are not spending all that time and effort with your leaders to stop the Europe-bound flow of people like you for nothing. No one is saying don't ever travel, but knowing your place means realising that to travel, you need a compelling reason. You are not an American or European who just finishes school, decides "I want to see the world" and books a ticket online, and takes off. This is the most important rule of all and you will find this coming up a lot as we move forward.

A good African knows that migration is a dirty word

Migration is a dirty, dirty word. Migration causes instability. No right-thinking, good African would wake up and decide they want to move to another continent. I know Americans and Europeans do this, but it is mostly to help people and all. Who will you be helping when you decide to abandon your country? What value will you be adding to Europe or America?

Why would you see a politically and economically stable country and just decide you want to move there? A good

African does not allow the things of this world to determine their choices in life. I know, I know. You are thinking you are a professional who will not be a burden and you just want to exercise your right to movement, blah blah blah. Those are not rights a good African should desire or contemplate. Contentment is a virtue. And a good African is virtuous.

A good African doesn't complain about paperwork

A good African does not ask why they are required to produce or sign a certain document. If it is on a list, a good African produces it without complaining. A good African is truthful and doesn't have creases on their forehead when answering the questions: "Are you a member of a terrorist organisation?", "Have you ever been involved with torturing someone?", "Are you coming to our awesome country to engage in prostitution?", "Have you ever been involved with human trafficking?", or "Do you plan to engage in espionage activities while in our awesome country?"

A good African does not covet humans that do not belong to him/her

To be clear, all love is not the same. Some types of love are regular, while others lead to severe and official consequences. The latter can lead to paperwork that can radically affect your ability to travel, thereby subverting the necessary process of verifying good Africans. Do not covet this extreme consequence. I am not implying that you want to do a fake marriage. I know you believe in love and all, but I am saying you shouldn't risk being associated with bad people. And isn't there a nice African you can marry?

A good African does not try to settle abroad, especially outside Africa

As a good African, you must provide proof that you have no intention of staying one minute beyond the period of grace as specified on your visa. One way of doing this is by making sure you always have your return ticket with you at all times. Don't be proud. You are not an American or European who can just travel and decide on a whim when they want to return. Not knowing exactly when and how you will return is bad and is a sign that you are one of those dangerous Africans who sneak away upon landing in Europe or America and try to stay there forever, ruining a country that took a lot of time, blood and energy to make perfect.

A good African discourages other Africans from spoiling chances for other good Africans

You must frequently speak up against those bad Africans who smuggle themselves onto boats or through deserts and spoil things for people like you. Regularly refer to the Khartoum Process. Write against Africans who give you a bad name. Embassies should be able to read that you are of the opinion that dangerous Africans who try to settle do not represent you. Say occasionally that Africans who have somehow settled abroad should come back home and stop embarrassing the rest of us good Africans who need to travel for conferences and training and medical treatment and short holidays.

A good African always comes back home

No one can read your mind. You must prove that you will return home by swearing that you have strong family and economic ties to the country where you belong to for life. It is nicer if you have a wife and many children who you could never abandon because you are a child of God. And a nice bank account that shows that you are not poor or anything. Sometimes, however, coming back home is not sufficient. Depending on what country you travelled to, you may be required to write to the kind embassy that granted you the privilege of travelling, telling them that, as you swore in the beginning, you are truly back in your country avoiding all temptation that may have come from bad Africans abroad. The temptation was great, but you had given them your word. And the word of a good African is their bond.

SAVIOURS LOCAL AND INTERNATIONAL

Our donors, who art abroad, hallowed be thy purse. Thy aid come in dollars and pounds. Thy will be done in our countries, as promoted by Bono. Give us this day, our yearly funding. And lead us not into self-reliance. But deliver us from ourselves. For thine are dollars, the pounds and the euros, forever and ever. Amen

HOW TO RUN A NIGERIAN NGO

The world is full of ungrateful people. People who cannot see beyond the small mercies to the big picture. People who are unnecessarily critical when they should see the bright side. Such people question the efficacy of NGOs, for example, and criticise them for standing in the way of real solutions. They say that government should provide services like health and education and that government should be held accountable when it doesn't do that. Why waste time on social struggles and accountability from government when you can just start an NGO? You must never listen to those people who question the existence of NGOs. What Nigeria, and indeed Africa, needs is an increase in projects. The best time to start an NGO is yesterday. The next best time is now.

The rules of the hustle

As a Nigerian you know the deal, everything is a hustle: government, politics, religion, all a hustle. The Nigerian God only helps those who help themselves. The key to survival is to understand the rules of the hustle so that by strategically positioning yourself, God can meet you at the point of your need and bless your project.

This is where the NGO comes in.

You hear that millions of dollars have been set aside by foreign governments and donors for development in Nigeria. Smile. It may be a hustle for them too, but the fact is they are really doing it because they love you. Don't wait to hear on radio or TV how this money is being spent. This will be unwise. You need to strategically position yourself now.

Get a lawyer to register your NGO at the Corporate Affairs Commission. Do your research before you do this. Find out what major donors such as the European Union, DFID, the UN and USAID have agreed to fund for the next few years. Avoid things that have received much funding in the past few years. Donors can be like children, they get bored with one thing and without warning, move to another. Plus, there is that evil thing threatening to truncate Europe's hustle called a recession. Although God is faithful and will protect your hustle from truncation, God also helps those who help themselves.

Millions of dollars have been set aside by donors. Smile.

You will need to take proactive steps to avoid being left with a redundant NGO due to lack of funding. Do one of two things: One, give your NGO a broad name that can cover two or more areas. The more the merrier. So instead of registering HIV/AIDS Alliance, register Health Watch Alliance. Instead of registering Alliance against Torture, register Alliance for the Protection of Human Rights. That way if there isn't much torture for you to benefit from, you can benefit from other human rights abuses.

On the other hand, you can register multiple NGOs. With this you can never go wrong. Always be willing and able to change the dance as soon as the donors change their tune.

Funding value

When building the foundations of your NGO, you must be careful about the kind of people you invite. You don't want the type who will suddenly become wild when the aid dollars start flowing in. Make the Board of Trustees your relatives and the parents of your close friends who are too busy, too old or too rich to care how you run your NGO. Include one neutral, fairly well-known person who has funding value: someone donors can respect. This person will be on the face of all your proposals.

Invest in media equipment: cameras, video recorders, projectors. Have pictures and videos to go with your proposals and letters of introduction. People need to see that you have been working hard, donating things and doing campaigns in your chosen field. Make sure you get lots of pictures of poor, sick-looking children you have helped. Or homeless people you have given blankets to.

Make friends with guys who work in donor agencies. Networking in the NGO world is important. Many times, crucial information about funding and projects slips out at social gatherings. This is how you know who is funding what and when.

A good proposal is everything

Take your time to work on proposals. A good proposal is everything. Seventy percent of the job of an NGO is paperwork — proposals and budgets and retirements and press releases. If you are not sure how to package an NGO proposal, learn. If you can't do it, don't be stingy. Pay someone to do it. Pay for a beautiful website with lots of photos showing things you are committed to. Foreign donors get tickled by nice functional websites. Make sure you visit the website of your donor and follow the guidelines strictly.

Usually a career in one of the big international donor agencies or NGOs will prepare you for all of the above. If you have the patience, look for a job with one of the UN agencies, DFID or USAID. Study their processes. In a few years you will be ready to become a big local consultant or start your own NGO.

Running an NGO can be tricky. You rely on the hustle of foreign and local donors. You can suddenly run dry. You do not get a pension. So, you must save for the day when donor rains cease to fall or you are too old to get another job. You must learn how to weave in extra items into the budget and inflate project costs. Anyone who calls this stealing, God will swiftly truncate their hustle.

When you spend donor money, you need to show that you really deserve it. So, if money is left over, you need to find a way to spend that money, otherwise the following year, you will get much less than you ask for.

Freedom of Information

As you run your NGO never assume that you will spend most of the money on actual causes. Don't get ahead of yourself. Preparation is key. Best is to spend up to 70% arranging meetings, paying admin and other overhead costs that will make sure that some of the remaining 30% of the funds you have goes to the cause where your hustle is domiciled.

Am I too technical? Let me give you a practical example. Say you run an organisation called the "Freedom of Information Alliance." Donors give you 100,000 dollars to promote Freedom of Information in Nigeria. Instead of squandering the whole amount actually promoting Freedom of Information in practical ways, thus wasting the money of kind donors, you must set aside considerable amounts for advocacy meetings (lunch and tea breaks included), a conference or seminar to discuss the issue, capacity building (I'm not sure what that means but you shouldn't think too hard about it either) and admin costs (some of the money should go to offsetting your rent in the heart of the city where rent is super expensive). With the rest, you can promote Freedom of Information. You can, for example, make a nice glossy booklet that says that Freedom of Information is important.

Cooperation

Now, say there is another NGO that does the same thing. Yes, that happens. Sometimes another person, somewhere, is thinking the exact same thing you are thinking. Or maybe they just overheard you in a barbershop or hair salon talking about your interests and decided to copy you.

You must never work together. I know sometimes donors will require coalitions on some issues. In those instances, endure it. Join the coalition for the purpose of accessing funds and looking good. But when it comes to your day to day work, ignore the rival NGO. Nothing good can come from sharing ideas or working together. People just want to steal your ideas and get all the money from donors.

People should understand that you can't risk clashing with your donor.

Sometimes, a situation may come up that needs you to look outside the narrowly defined grants that donors give. Well, it is not your fault that people's problems don't align with the specific proposal you made to the donor. The thing is, God can see your heart and you really want to do what is right. Of course, you would like to help people with real problems, if you could. But people should understand that you can't risk clashing with your donor. How will you be able to afford rent for your nice office?

People need to be reasonable in their expectations. You are, after all, the only alternative to corrupt, inefficient government. What would anyone do without you?

Gratitude

Remember that the local people you are trying to help have no idea what they want. If they did, they wouldn't need you in the first place. If you say they need Freedom of Information, then that is what they need. If you say they need a borehole, then what they need is a borehole. There is no need to spend time asking the people on the ground how they would do things. Often, they will be too grateful for what you have done for them to bother about the effectiveness of your intervention. And that is all that matters: their gratitude.

Because NGO people are jealous, it is important that as God blesses your NGO hustle, you do not draw attention to yourself. You don't want fellow NGO people reporting you to the Economic and Financial Crimes Commission. Wear casual shirts (preferably sewn with kampala fabric) on jeans unless you are attending donor meetings or meetings with government counterparts. No need to advertise all the money you are making from saving your fellow countrymen.

Never miss dinners and meetings organised by embassies and donors. These people are an important link to funding. It doesn't matter if you do not get a personal invitation, once there is 'civil society' in the program, polish your shoes, take your glossy complimentary cards and get going.

Get some street credibility

If you are into human rights, try to get arrested. Foreign donors get excited when they meet human rights activists who have actually been locked up or who have gory tales to tell. Take advantage of popular protests to boost your activist CV and the reputation of your NGO. You don't want to take this too far however. The idea is to get attention, not get killed or locked up indefinitely. Be smart.

Do television, radio and newspaper interviews. Pay to get interviewed if possible. It is for the cause. Do press releases. You must not only do work but be seen to do work. The more visible you are, the more NGO points you get. The more NGO points you get, the more funding you are likely to continue to have.

One final thing: when in doubt, remember the three W's:
1. What would the donors do?
2. What do the donors want?
3. What can the donors fund?

If you follow my advice, before long, you will be flying from one all-expenses-paid foreign conference and seminar to another. All for the cause. May you continue to receive funding and may God, through your NGO, bless your hustle.

HOW TO BE A BLACK SAVIOUR

Look, I have been reading all the woke literature and websites (so you don't have to) and I can tell you, white saviours are a travesty. They are everywhere in your face from international NGOs to lead characters in movies that should be about black people. Let me quickly say before you begin to think of a solution that involves any sort of reform of these bad individuals: White saviours are beyond redemption, as useless as a pot that has been used to boil pepper soup to a person who wants to boil bathing water. No matter how much you wash that pot, you will still feel the pepper in your eyes and privates.

You must look inward, to discover the saviour in you. You must become a black saviour, the single most important tool in the fight against the scourge of the white saviour complex. (In this piece of advice I will use "BS", "the black saviour" and "black saviours" interchangeably). God bless the black saviour.

Allow me to introduce the black saviour to you.

Relative to the average hopeless, poverty-stricken citizen, the black saviour stands in a position of privilege. They live abroad, shielded from typhoid, malaria, fuel queues, too-hot-for-sex weather, state sanctioned homophobia, shameless politicians and killer soldiers. Some have recently returned from living abroad following epiphanies of how desperately the country needs their expertise, talent, and superior foreign currency. Some might maliciously imply that, of these returnees, most are fleeing harsh economic conditions, foreigners they have impregnated or defrauded, taxes or the law, but it is wrong to judge the intentions of Man. That is the work of God. And God does not treat usurpers kindly.

The easiest identifying characteristic of the black saviour is an intense hatred for the white saviour. The black saviour would beat the white saviour with a tree trunk if he caught him in a forest where assault was not against the law. More importantly, the black saviour has as the singular goal in life; protecting the black man from the white saviour.

Some black saviours, after being persecuted on the basis of their political beliefs or sexuality, have gotten asylum in white countries. Some others, all thanks to their parents, were born in white countries and are citizens of those countries. They are in the vanguard of the protection of black dignity and rights. Like when that blue-eyed busybody went and (some say "innocently", but like black saviours I don't care) raised millions of dollars to fight an African warlord (Kony of the Lord's Resistance Army) that we had all forgotten about. For all we know Kony could be pining away from syphilis in some forest. Thank God that black saviours jumped in and criticised that white madness. Next time he will think before trying to save black people from themselves.

The black saviour usually writes from abroad, taking the time out of a busy schedule comprising two to four jobs, to moan about how bad the country is, how things must change, how we must reject the influence of white saviours in our insane countries. I imagine BS hunched over laptops, iPads and tea (or coffee, I hear they all love coffee once they go abroad) and ridiculously fast internet connections typing furiously about the state of the nation, human rights, our 'inchoate' publishing industry or bad white guys. This isn't easy. I salute their courage.

Once in a while, black saviours may even brave the cold and hold a placard outside the Nigerian embassy in their sane country of residence. Now it is important to note that just like Jesus warned about imposters who would perform miracles in his name, not everyone carrying a placard in the name of Nigeria in a white country is a black saviour. We must be vigilant. Now, how do we know who is a real one? Sometimes, after returning from a long stay abroad, the black saviours may have what I have christened Sane Country Withdrawal Syndrome (SCWS). This is a serious ailment and all decent people must show empathy. The Sane Country Withdrawal Syndrome (SCWS) is an imperceptible bastard that creeps up on the true black saviour without a big announcement. I have however studied the symptoms. After a few years of returning, (during which time the foreign accent may or may not be lost, this depends on how early the parents intervened to save their child from the insane nation of his or her birth) the black saviour is still shocked at how things are done "in this country". You will hear things like "When I was in Cincinnati", "This how we used do it in Brussels" or "This is tosh! The British would never do this" in every bit of conversation. SCWS does not allow the black saviour to ever feel at home in his own country. There is a resultant irritation and frustration that becomes worse upon the traumatic realisation that it has become impossible to go back to the white country. In my prayers I will reserve a minute every day for BS living with SCWS. Because I care.

It is my hope that you can save your country and generation from having to depend on white saviours obsessed with fixing the world, by choosing the noble path of the black saviour. May the good lord who sees your large heart, increase your capacity for salvation and bless your glorious black saviour hustle.

WHEN IN NIGERIA…

NOTES FOR THE FOREIGNER IN NIGERIA

HOW TO BE AN EXPATRIATE IN NIGERIA

I have always held that the Nigerian God is far too kind. Kind to our political leaders in spite of their wickedness, kind to our religious leaders in spite of their hypocrisy, kind to our traditional leaders in spite of their complicity in all the mess we find ourselves in. And kinder to white foreigners. I mean, you can be a technician from the roughest, poorest parts of the London Borough of Tower Hamlets and suddenly become a foreign engineer with servants, a huge salary and a secure mansion in the best parts of Abuja. We are in awe of white expatriates.

You have left hardship, harsh winters and a horrible economic recession in your nice developed country and are now an economic refugee in Nigeria. Of course, we don't know this; you are the expat who will save us from ruin and teach us how things ought to be done. You have gotten a job with an organisation or company which has applied for expatriate quota for you and secured nice accommodation with a generator, a car and a driver. You have said goodbye to your family and friends and moved to Nigeria. Maybe you have even come with Hector, your cat. God will bless you for choosing our country. I mean you could have ended up in small Togo but you came here. This is how you must conduct yourself while living in Nigeria.

As soon as you arrive get in contact with other expatriates.

There are online groups and you will quickly find whatever it is you need, from stores that sell foreign food to people selling off their furniture and books.

You are here to work and live large, not contaminate yourself with the locals. You can enjoy this country while pretending to live in your own country. Identify hangout spots that are "expat joints". Your expat friends will tell what joints are suitable for expats, joints with food so expensive it scares the locals away. If there are any locals you can be sure they are in the safe upper classes. You don't want to go and catch some deadly disease like malaria or dengue fever. Do nice expat things like jogging with fellow foreigners through the nice safe streets of Abuja and having a nice picnic after. Of course, there will be the odd local but that is ok. Makes it nice and colourful.

When you are able to muster the courage to go to a non-expat joint, come in groups and dance with each other in a corner. The important thing is you have done something revolutionary: risked kidnapping by going to an unprotected joint. Have a local guide — a nice junior member of staff from the office who understands the pecking order. Drink as much as you can and party as often as you can. Where else in this messed-up global economy can you enjoy this much luxury?

Do not learn a local language. What's the point?

Complain about everything in the country. Complain about how you can never find the kind of cat food that your cat, Hector, enjoys. Complain about how nobody cares about animals. Talk about how rude the locals are and how sloppy everyone is. Complain about how bad the driving is and how loud (except if you are American) everyone is. Complain about how nothing works in this country, about the heat, the slow and expensive internet service. Because, in your cold, civilized, recession-hit country, everything works.

Have a nice upper-class local couple who can agree with you when you talk about how horrible things are. Invite them for dinner occasionally. This proves you are cool with the locals and are not racist. Also, occasionally invite those who may not be upper class, but who consider themselves progressives, the cultural elite. People who have read the books you have read and can talk about art from your country. They may drink all your alcohol and eat more ravenously than your upper-class couple, but the conversation will be worth it.

Avoid the local food. Something terrible will happen to you if you eat the local food that is so low in nutrition and high in cholesterol and bacteria. Hire a cook who knows how to make food from your country.

Expect the locals to respect your culture even though you are in their country. It is ok to dress inappropriately — after all in your country, you are a free to wear whatever you like, or nothing at all.

I hope that you enjoy Nigeria and slowly get used to the heat and the reports of explosions and violence. Not to worry, you are safe. When we kill each other we usually leave out the foreigners. And the guys who used to kidnap foreigners are busy with more official duties. Stay well and God bless your foreign hustle.

TIPS FOR THE FOREIGN JOURNALIST COVERING NIGERIAN ELECTIONS

Nigeria is an important country for many reasons. First there is the jihadist group Boko Haram which has engaged in an expansionist campaign, freaking out everyone in the free world. Then there is the fact that Nigeria is Africa's largest economy. Sometimes. So, understandably, when we have elections as we have managed to do without break since 1999, it sparks interest in many Nigeria watchers around the world. From those who arrive with predictions of mayhem and violence, packing with them a bullet-proof vest and hopes for a big break reporting from a hot crisis area, to those who take advantage of no one from their little European country wanting to do this job, everyone needs tips from the locals.

Yes you will have to endure the irritation of getting a visa: a small gift of reciprocity for all the countries where Nigerians suffer indignities trying to get visas. That is the only difficult part. Just follow the advice here and you will have an amazing time.

NOTE: Most of my advice is for the white or light-skinned foreigner. If you are black and cannot be visibly identified as a foreigner, then I am sorry, you will have to work as hard as every other local journalist.

There is no protocol for the foreign journalist.

You may think, I want to interview a high-profile politician and I am not sure a foreigner who just flew in to cover the elections will be able to get access. Nonsense! There are no access issues for the foreign journalist in Nigeria. You know the saying "man proposes, God disposes"? Well, here it is "foreign journo proposes, foreign journo disposes". Especially if you are white, there is hardly any door you cannot walk right through and be greeted with a smile. If you cannot enter, then rest assured that no one can.

You are white. Embrace it.

Like I said above, this article is for the light(er)-skinned journalist. In Nigeria, all light-skinned foreigners are referred to as white, or "oyinbo". Up north, where Hausa is the main language, you will be called "bature". It does not matter if you are Algerian, Mexican or Chinese. Do not try to argue or explain that you are not white. The tag comes with a lot of perks like the one in 1. above. You will experience more love and attention than you have ever received since the nurse first showed you to your parents.

Don't be shy to ask personal questions

Sure there are taboo questions, but because you are foreign, most of these will not apply to you. Do not be shocked if you find people telling you their most intimate secrets. You will not need to be very influential for a public official to share sensitive government information or for a random stranger to tell you the crimes they have committed. There is something about your skin that makes us trust you. Milk it.

Prepare for the beer gardens

Especially in Lagos and Abuja, you will find that there are dozens of beer gardens or bush bars in any one area. Feel free to explore these lively places but please do not wear those hideous brown khaki shorts that foreign journos like to wear in tropical countries. Along with the general population, mosquitoes converge there and will not hesitate to feast on you. Especially you. If you have never had malaria before, trust me, the first time is not good. Plus, you don't want to be delirious with fever while your colleagues are out covering electoral violence. An African election report without some violence is like a man with erectile dysfunction. You don't want that.

Love is a dangerous game

Everyone needs some loving. While you are in Nigeria, there is nothing wrong in some adventure of a sexual nature. Again, it doesn't matter how you look — old, fat, sun-burnt — you will be treated like a local celebrity. Sex (transactional and otherwise) will be fairly easy to find. People will tell you very quickly that you are beautiful, or even, that they love you. Especially if you are no longer in your prime and it has been years since someone last said those words to you, it can be quite intoxicating to hear them. Enjoy the attention, but be careful. You may end up sponsoring someone's trip abroad. Love at your own risk.

The gay shall [not] inherit the [Nigerian] earth

If you are gay and you need some action while you are in Nigeria, you might want to be extra cautious. It is a crime to show any same sex amorous affection. We can talk about how this is against human rights and all another time. Today it is a crime, and you can get in trouble. Plus, the open playing field for the gay foreigner in Nigeria is a minefield. To scam you, we will pretend to be gay. Don't use the internet for hook-ups. I am not recommending abstinence (that can be frustrating), but you might want to think about it.

We stare at foreigners. Deal with it.

You will find out very quickly that as a white foreigner, you stand out. People will stare at you, nonstop. No, they will not look away when you look back. Yes, they will call out to you in the streets, referring to you by race. Calm down. This is not racist. It is endearment. Deal with it.

You will pay more. Think of it as reparations.

Will you be charged higher prices when you go to the market or take cabs or pay for sex? Yes. Yes. Yes. Triple! If you ask me, it is a small price to pay for all that love. Deal with it.

The devil is in the spices

Especially if you are from places with bland food, the first time you eat a Nigerian dish will be followed by reactions that will require a long period of recovery. If you do not like hot spices, you might want to mention that several times before the food arrives.

Vegans can go to hell

I am sorry but if you are vegan, food will be a challenge for you here. If you will not feel too guilty about it, you might want to take a vegan break in Nigeria and enjoy the meaty culinary delights for the one or two weeks you will be here. Trust me, the one or two kilos of meat you will eat in the period will not destroy the planet. However, to deal with any extreme guilt when you do go back home, you can volunteer at a homeless shelter, donate to Oxfam or to one of those animal rights organisations.

I hope you enjoy Nigeria as much as I hope Nigeria enjoys you.

APPENDIX AND TRAVEL ADVICE

TRAVEL ADVICE FOR NIGERIANS GOING TO THE U.S.

The Ministry of Foreign Affairs of the Federal Republic of Nigeria warns Nigerian citizens of the continuing risks of travel to the U.S. and recommends that Nigerian citizens avoid all travel to Arkansas, California, Idaho, Mississippi, Missouri, Nevada, New Jersey, Texas, Tennessee, and Wisconsin because of the large number of hate groups and/or the situation in those states being fluid and unpredictable. Due to the persistent threat of domestic terrorism by lone white wolves with mental health issues, the Nigerian government restricts travel by Nigerian government personnel to all areas where civilian Americans are allowed to freely purchase automatic firearms and limits the activities of Nigerian government and personnel and their family members while in New York, Atlanta, and Houston. (To be clear, they have guns and they kill people, especially black people.)

The Federal Government strongly urges Nigerian citizens in the U.S. to consider their personal security and to keep personal safety in the forefront of their travel planning. We know some of you who are very light-skinned or even mixed-race may think you will be exempt from this hate against black people. (This from years of being fondly called oyinbo in Nigeria.) You are sorely mistaken. In America anyone who is not 100% white is black. You are black. They will kill you if they catch you. We have warned you.

The ability of the Federal Government to provide assistance to Nigerian citizens in Alaska, Arkansas, Idaho, Missouri, Mississippi, New Jersey, Tennessee, Wisconsin, and Wyoming remains severely limited.

The Federal Government continues to recommend against all but essential travel to the following states due to the risk of police shootings and brutality, drug gangs, racist attacks, white nationalists (Nazis), unhealthy fast food linked to obesity and diabetes, measles and anti-vaxxers, people who go on Jerry Springer, drive-by shootings, violence on black Friday, Donald Trump, Trump supporters and other similar dangerous things: Texas, Oklahoma, Georgia, Baltimore, Iowa, Michigan, Pennsylvania, Louisiana, Virginia, Kentucky, New York, Washington DC, Alabama, South Carolina, Arkansas, Utah, Idaho, Wyoming. The Federal Government also retains the warning from the previous travel advisory against travel in Ferguson because of the threat of riots and police whose basic gear resembles that of the army — we are not sure that much has changed. Worse, Ferguson has an armed group of white people called the Oath Keepers whose self-imposed mandate is to "defend the Constitution against all enemies, foreign and domestic" and who normally show up when black people are protesting. Basically, white people protecting white people with high-calibre guns. The Federal Government cannot explain this. Just stay safe and out of Ferguson. The Federal Government also extends this warning to Charlottesville, Virginia where the risk is high from armed white racists addicted to confederate statues. Do not go to Charlottesville.

Based on safety and security risk assessments, the Embassy maintains restrictions for travel by Nigerian officials to those states listed above (and all other states with significant numbers of Trump supporters); officials must receive advance clearance by the Nigerian Mission for any travel deemed as mission-essential. Nigerian citizens should be aware that extremists could expand their operations beyond the south, mid-west and President Donald Trump's strongholds and hotels to other areas of the country.

The Nigerian Mission advises all Nigerian citizens to be particularly vigilant around traffic lights, police vehicles, rallies full of white people (whether armed or not), white neighbourhoods (white people call the police when they see black people), Americans who refuse to vaccinate their children; locations where large crowds of black people may gather (as this may attract white police, Molotov cocktails, tear gas and murderous white nationalists). Security measures in the U.S. remain heightened due to threats posed by racist groups, Trump supporters, I.C.E. and the police in general. Since an extremist police group killed Michael Brown in August 2014, over 1,000 persons have been killed by police throughout the country. Do not say we didn't warn you. Sometimes they kill you by choking you to death, breaking your spinal cord behind a police van, hanging you in a police cell and calling it a suicide or just shooting you point blank as you are reaching for your seat belt or playing with a toy gun. And definitely no toy guns.

2014–17 and beyond saw an increase in deaths by police in the U.S.. Although several hashtags went viral on the internet, police continued their killing without fear that the whole world could be watching. Sometimes, it didn't matter that passers-by were filming the police brutality. These people just pull the trigger and explain later.

President Donald Trump continues to threaten that he will be harsh with immigration. Nigerians may find themselves at the receiving end of this. While the Federal Government's prayers against the tragedy of Mr. Trump becoming president went largely unanswered, the Embassy continues to assure Nigerians that it will continue to respond to threats from President Donald Trump as much as it can. However, hold your return ticket just in case as there is no in-flight entertainment on flights specially meant for deportation.

Again, the U.S. makes it shockingly easy to purchase a gun. Even a person with a record of crime or mental illness can buy a gun. They love guns. This means that someone who hates Mondays can walk out of his or her house and go on a shooting spree in a school. The Federal Government cannot explain Americans' love for guns. Be vigilant at all times. Someone whose girlfriend broke up with them may just shoot you.

Violent crimes occur throughout the country. Law enforcement authorities usually respond harshly especially when you are black (again it does not matter how light-skinned you are). A word is enough for the wise.

TRAVEL ADVICE FOR NIGERIANS GOING TO THE UK

The Federal Republic of Nigeria, aware of the strategic importance of the United Kingdom's health care system to the survival of its political class and elite, but equally aware of its general duty to Nigerians travelling to the United Kingdom, reluctantly offers the following travel advice, without prejudice to its gratitude and dependence.

The United Kingdom is addicted to knives. Knife attacks and stabbings can happen suddenly and without warning, on busses, on trains, in the streets, in parks, in hotels. Do not carry a knife on you for any reason and if you have to purchase a kitchen knife, do so quickly, carry it in a bag and have your receipt on hand to show it to the police.

The United Kingdom is the spiritual home of football hooliganism and large groups of inebriated young men — often with no hope for the future and a total dependence on this way of life for any self-respect — go about armed with the crudest of tools on match days looking for a fight. Avoid large groups of British men, especially when they are singing songs.

Football supporters are the equivalent of gang members, so carefully research what area you wear which football jersey to. If you can, avoid football jerseys altogether.

Credible information received by the Federal Government indicates that terrorist groups continue to plot possible attacks in Europe. All European countries remain potentially vulnerable to attacks from transnational terrorist organisations. The UK Security Service, commonly known as MI5, publishes specific reasons for any changes in the threat level and recommended actions for the public via its UK threat levels website. While this may seem to pale in comparison to terrorist threats in Nigeria like Boko Haram or herdsmen or corrupt politicians, the Federal Government must WARN Nigerians against being overconfident. Death is death, whether by Boko Haram bombs or by a terrorist who eats fish and chips.

The Federal Government wants to warn in detail about the potential for isolated violence related to the political situation in Northern Ireland. But really why would any Nigerian need to be in Northern Ireland? In short, don't go there. The ability of the Federal Government to help those who end up there remains severely limited.

Avoid areas of demonstrations if possible, and be careful within the vicinity of demonstrations or the vicinity of pubs. The British drink and they drink until they get violent. Even demonstrations intended to be peaceful can turn confrontational and possibly escalate to violence. Stay current with media coverage of local events and be aware of your surroundings.

Big cities in the UK are a bit like Lagos. So:

Be cautious and aware of your surroundings. Not every black person is your brother.

Be vigilant: pickpocketing, "snatch and grab" theft of mobile phones, watches and jewellery can occur. Like in Lagos. The only thing that doesn't happen here is stealing of private parts.

Be alert to other criminal schemes, such as impostors posing as undercover police officers and "fining" tourists for bogus minor offences. A legitimate Metropolitan Police Services officer will never demand an immediate cash payment. This is not Nigeria.

When you catch a thief you are not allowed to beat them to death, unlike in Nigeria. You may restrain them while they are doing the stealing but no, you can't kill them. The Federal Government will not offer assistance if you choose to commit murder.

Use only licensed Black Cabs or pre-ordered car services (minicabs). Unlicensed taxis or private cars posing as taxis may offer low fares, but in some instances, travellers have been robbed or sexually assaulted while using these cars. The Safer Travel at Night partnership among the Metropolitan Police, Transport for London, and the Mayor of London maintains a website with additional information on cabs and car services.

Avoid using ATMs that look temporary in structure or location or are located in isolated areas — they may not be legitimate. Use ATMs located inside a bank branch.

Scams: Before sending any money to individuals you have never met in person, visit the Embassy's UK website for more information about internet financial scams and how to protect yourself. Financial crimes conducted over the internet have increased dramatically in the United Kingdom as scammers attempt to convince you to send them money. (It would be a real shame for a Nigerian to be scammed in the UK!)

COMMON NIGERIAN PHRASES AND EXPRESSIONS

"I want your honest opinion" = Keep your unflattering opinions to yourself. Shower me with praise and adulation. Preferably something I can quote.

"I am coming" (except when said during intercourse) = I am leaving. Goodbye.

"I am almost there" = When I finish heating the water to take my bath I will run just one small errand and then head to where you are.

"With all due respect" = I am about to go to great lengths to undermine, insult and disrespect you. Please don't act like a child and take it personally.

"I will not take much of your time" = Forgive me and my insensitivity. Brace yourself for a long and rambling speech.

"I will be brief" = You are about to regret letting me speak. This will last a long time.

"I don't want to repeat what has just been said" = I am about to repeat what has just been said.

"Laps" = Lap.

"God-willing/ By the grace of God/Insha Allah" = These expressions have no known meaning. It is safe to disregard.

"I concur" = I pretend to agree. But it is important to allow me to use another set of words to say the same thing.

"To God who made me/ I swear to God" = My only witness in this matter is busy in heaven. So I might as well lie to you.

"Wetin you born?" = Tell me the gender of your child so that I can formulate an appropriate response. e.g. "Eiya", "Is that?" or "Praise God".

"Who do you think you are?" = Quickly establish if you are or know someone who can cause great suffering in my life, so I know whether to fight you or leave you in the hands of God.

"Do you know who I am?" = Do you realise that I could know or be someone in government who can cause great suffering in your life?

"Why you dey do like woman?" = This is inappropriate for a male human. (More recently= dude, you are gay).

"Moks"= Mosque.

"Aks"= Ask.

"Dress" = Move over/ Make space for me.

"Where are you from/What tribe are you?" = There is no time to waste. I need to know quickly if I should trust or hate you.

"Severally (as in, I called you severally)" = Several times.

"I am a detribalised Nigerian" = I do not peddle my hatred for other tribes in public.

"Tea" = This includes most instant beverages that are drunk in the morning, e.g. Bournvita, Milo, Coffee.

"Omo" = Powder Detergent. There are different types of omo e.g. Ariel, So Klin, Omo.

"Maggi" = Seasoning cubes. There are different types of maggi e.g. Knorr, Royco, Maggi.

Transforming a manuscript into the book you are now reading is a team effort. Cassava Republic Press would like to thank everyone who helped in the production of *Be(com)ing Nigerian: A Guide*

Editorial
Bibi Bakare-Yusuf
Layla Mohamed
Yomi Olusunle

Design & Production
Seyi Adegoke
Tobi Ajiboye

Sales & Marketing
Kofo Okunola
Emma Shercliff

Publicity
Lynette Lisk

Our efforts would also be fruitless without our buyers and readers who continue to support and reward us. And for that, all of us at Cassava Republic Press would like to thank you.